ERITREA REMEMBERED

Recollections & Photos by Peace Corps Volunteers

edited by Marian Haley Beil

A PEACE CORPS WRITERS BOOK

A PEACE CORPS WRITERS BOOK.
An imprint of Peace Corps Worldwide.

ERITREA REMEMBERED: RECOLLECTIONS & PHOTOS BY PEACE CORPS VOLUNTEERS.
All stories are copyrighted by the authors. All rights reserved.
Printed in the United States of America by Peace Corps Writers of Oakland, California,
a component of PeaceCorpsWorldwide.org.
No part of this book may be used or reproduced in any manner whatsoever
without written permission except in the case of brief quotations
contained in critical articles or reviews.

Disclaimer: This book is not an official Peace Corps publication.
The opinions expressed herein are those of the authors
and they alone are responsible for the contents of this book.

For more information, contact peacecorpsworldwide@gmail.com.
Peace Corps Writers and the Peace Corps Writers colophon are trademarks of Peace Corps Worldwide.

All photographs provided by the authors except where noted.
Cover photos (left to right, top to bottom): *front cover* — Kate Yocum with two of her students, Kudo-Abour;
students in a classroom, Assab (from Richard Beal); students at school, Kudo-Abour.
back cover — Lois Shoemaker with children at the Itegue Menen Hospital Orphanage, Asmara;
Paul Huntsberger and his welcoming committee, Saganeiti;
Mary Gratiot Schultz with the family of her student, Kesete Gebrekristos;
at the wedding of Hamilton and Joanne Feldman Richards, Keren;
Paul Huntsberger and his maid and Eritrean mother, Berekti Andu, Saganeiti;
Marianne Arieux and students from the Itegue Menen Dresser School, Asmara, depart for visit to a clinic in the countryside.
Scorpion illustration on page 121 from *Where There Is No Doctor* by David Werner with Carol Thuman and Jane Maxwell,
published by the Hesperian Foundation, publishers of health care books for rural communities around the world.
Copy editor: Martha Haley
Book design: Marian Haley Beil

Library of Congress Control Number: 2011944267

ISBN-13: 978-1-935925-16-3
ISBN-10: 1935925164

FIRST PEACE CORPS WRITERS EDITION, December 2011

FOR OUR ERITREAN FRIENDS

Table of Contents

Asmara

Decamere

2011 MARKS THE 50TH ANNIVERSARY of the Peace Corps. What started as a suggestion by President John F. Kennedy during a campaign stop at the University of Michigan in 1960, quickly materialized into reality during the first year of his presidency when 51 Peace Corps Volunteers left the United States for Ghana. Since then 200,000 Volunteers have served in 139 countries. While their opportunities and challenges vary greatly, almost every Volunteer makes the same statement about his or her individual experience: "It changed my life."

This book is a brief collection of some words and images of the recollections of Peace Corps Volunteers who served in Eritrea in the Horn of Africa. Many of these Volunteers were eyewitnesses to the early stages of the Eritrean struggle for independence. These Volunteers and the hundreds of others who served in Eritrea in the 1960s, 1970s and in an independent Eritrea in the mid-1990s developed a great love and respect for the Eritrean people. The friendships and love developed in a few short years shaped the entire lifetime of many Volunteers.

To celebrate the 50th anniversary of the Peace Corps and to pay homage to our Eritrean friends we share here some of our stories and memories.

Adi Teclesan

A Brief Time in Adi Teclesan

BY WALT GALLOWAY (ADI TECLESAN 1970)

AS NEW PEACE CORPS VOLUNTEERS, my wife, Mary-Jean, and I were first assigned to teach at a school in Axum — a wonderful location with electricity, DC3 plane service everyday, and houses that looked like Italian villas thanks to the influence of the long Italian occupation of the province just to the north — Eritrea. Another benefit of being in Axum was that it was a long — but not too long — bus ride or a short hop by plane to Asmara — our "haven" that gave us respite from the challenges we faced in Axum. Often we went to Asmara for supplies, and these trips provided the chance to stay in the Harmasian, our favorite hotel, and to enjoy the good ferengi food that was readily available (Chicken in Rice Supreme Sauce!).

Our challenges in Axum arose from the fact that there was a relatively large group of Haile Selassie I University students assigned to the local schools as national service teachers. These students, who were informed about world events and knew what was happening in Vietnam, saw parallels in that conflict to what was happening with American military support being provided to the Ethiopian government — and they didn't like it. It became convenient for them to strike out at us as Americans. Though we agreed with their views and perceptions, we never had an opportunity to talk to them about the issues. Instead, they threw stones through our kitchen window as we sat having dinner one night, almost hitting our awesome maid, Yohannesu.

The wonderful Peace Corps support administrator for our area, Temesgen Araya, came to Axum from Asmara to evaluate the episode and spoke with many people in the community about our situation. Following that visit, we decided to stay. Things were quiet for a while. Some months later, however, as we were showing films requested by our students of the first moon landing, the students of the national service teachers stood outside and threw rocks on the tin roof of the school. That ended our time in Axum. Again with great support from Temesgen, we moved to Adi Teclesan.

The "Peace Corps house" in Adi Teclesan

ADI TECLESAN

We set up housekeeping in the "Peace Corps house" that had been occupied previously by Volunteers. It was right across the street from the school and the town well. Although there were only a few months left in the school year, we started to get to know our students and fellow teachers.

Prior to our arrival in Adi Teclesan the well had a pump that was run by windmill power. The system had been funded by USAID and built by U.S. Army troops from Kagnew Station in Asmara. But by the time we arrived the townspeople had disconnected the windmill because it was too unreliable. Instead they turned the wheel by hand to fill their buckets or canvas bags. We bought our water from a "water boy"

The boy who brought water

who fetched water from the well. He had a donkey that carried two large canvas water bags on each of its sides. The boy had the greatest smile.

We enjoyed Adi Teclesan. There were gorgeous birds living in the indigenous plants right around our house; there was a typical Coptic Christian church that stood on the highest hill in town; there were sod-roofed houses built into some of the hills that were very different from the houses in Axum.

We also became familiar with the small groups of women who danced and chanted through town to invoke rain (it was very dry there) and they actually did that with some success.

Because our house and the school were both right on the Keren Road, we became very familiar with military trucks transporting Ethiopian Army troops from Asmara to Keren, the center of fighting with the Eritrean Liberation Front. We also saw small bands of men, young and old alike, carrying firearms that appeared to be the same age as the owners (I think some of the guns would have exploded in their hands if they'd actually fired them). These men were in some way connected to the ELF, and there was occasional fighting not far from our village. In addition, a Peace Corps Volunteer from another town was kidnapped by the ELF as he travelled by the littorina from Asmara to Massawa.

Unfortunately, the sum of these circumstances resulted in a directive coming from Peace Corps/Ethiopia that required us to travel with a police escort whenever we went outside of Adi Teclesan — even the relatively short distance of less than 20 miles to Asmara. It was our feeling that having a police escort only served to draw attention to the fact that we were there. In the end, we decided it was best to depart Adi Teclesan, and sadly we did.

We were given the option of going home, or finding another location for our second year of Peace Corps service. We chose to stay in Ethiopia and moved far to the southwest to the much quieter land of Gemu Gofa at the very end of the DC3/C47 runs from Addis. We lived in Jinka in the middle of a coffee grove with papaya trees, but without electricity or glass in the windows.

It was a good, and relatively uneventful year in Gemu Gofa. It was totally different from Eritrea and Tigre, and made our Peace Corps experience all that much more valuable and enlightening.

Returning to Our Future

BY WAYNE KESSLER (ADI TECLESAN 1964–1966)

AS THE PLANE DESCENDED in the early morning light, déjà vu hit me squarely between the eyes. The Asmara airport looked exactly like it did 28 years before when Laurie and I first landed there to take up our Peace Corps teaching posts. Same buildings, same pastel green color, same morning light — it seemed that nothing had changed. I didn't know what to expect exactly, but I didn't think that I'd be stepping back in time either.

I had started seeing Eritreans from the U.S. and Europe in the boarding lounge at Heathrow. Eritreans and Ethiopians look very much alike so I resorted to walking up to one small group after another and asking, "Where are you going?" If they said, Asmara, I continued by asking more questions like, "Where do you live now? How long has it been since you've been back?" An older man wearing a Moslem turban who lived in Phoenix, Arizona, said "I last saw my family in 1968 when I went to field and joined the struggle. When I got ill, they sent me to Sudan and then to Canada. Canada was very cold so I moved to Arizona. Now I want to find my relatives." He was very proud of his four children who all were going to or had finished college. "Even the girls," he said with a huge smile despite the long sleepless flight from his adopted home.

All whom I talked to were returning for the first time since fleeing a despotic Ethiopian regime and leaving their families, some more than 20 years ago. They frequently referred to themselves as the diaspora. It was sad to learn that they were forced to leave, many of them walking hundreds of miles at night through deserts in Sudan. But in 1992, they were excited and proud of their country's newly won independence.

During the night flight, I sensed a sweet joyful tension as we headed toward Asmara — we all wondered, "Who will meet us? What will we see?"

During the night flight, I sensed a sweet joyful tension as we headed toward Asmara — we all wondered, "Who will meet us? What will we see?" Just before landing there was this buzz of hushed talk. Then, as we left the plane, the women trilled, then cried, sang, and rhythmically clapped their hands as they met their relatives. The men did so as well. I got caught up in the excitement, too. Some women even bent over and kissed the runway. When I saw our former colleagues Ghebrecristos and Ghebremicael and the others who were waiting for me, the thrill became deeply personal.

It was hard to believe that I was actually with them again, but the hubbub was real enough. "Mr. Wayne, welcome, welcome." "How are you? What about your neck?" (I had cervical fusion surgery just eleven days before departure.) "How is Mrs. Laurie? How are Colin and Mehret?" "We are happy to see you." Except for the neck question, all these were part of the typical greeting — everyone speaking at once and not really expecting immediate answers. My friends accompanied me to Ghebrecristos's house, where I would stay throughout my visit, and where his wife and daughter-in-law repeated the greetings, kissing me repeatedly on the cheeks. Lots of people came to see me, some of whom knew us from the past and many who simply wanted to see their first American. They were adjusting to me, just as I was adjusting to being with these good friends again — and to the 7,400-foot altitude.

Asmara

The next day, Ghebrecristos and I took a 30-year-old blue bus to the open-air market and walked toward Asmara's main street, just like old times. It was as if the whole city had a glass lid put over it for 30 years. Nothing looked like it had changed. The buildings were the same — same paint, same signs. There was the same Bar Royal where we enjoyed gelato and cappuccino sitting at sidewalk tables. It was astonishing. I knew just where to turn for the post office, the main bank, the Ministry of Education, and the public library, commonly called the "American Library" because it had been the United States Information Service library before. Asmara still looked like a southern Italian art deco style town with fading pastel colors and ornate window- and door-frames that were right out of the 1920s and '30s. Despite the war, there had been very little damage due to the fighting. I saw one old factory building that had bullet holes all over it, but Ghebrecristos told me, "That happened ten years before and they never repaired it."

Asmara still looked like a southern Italian art deco style town with fading pastel colors and ornate window- and door-frames that were right out of the 1920s and '30s.

And Asmara was clean. Early every morning hoards of sweepers moved across the city pushing antique wheelbarrows that carried brooms and shovels for cleaning the streets. Sometimes they swept sidewalks in slow broad strokes using palm fronds from the big trees lining the main street.

I could stand in the middle of the main street, look both directions, and see only three or four vehicles in a 10-block section.

But I was always in a crowd, leisurely strolling with people just enjoying their freedom and gathering with friends to visit and drink tea. We were walking in streets that had been previously off limits entirely or at least after evening curfew. Surprisingly — only nine months after a 30-year war — it was safe to walk around anywhere night or day.

Because Ghebrecristos was chief education officer for the province, he was always stopping to greet people, and I had to keep my camera in my left hand to be ready for all the handshaking. He delighted in introducing me to what seemed to be hundreds of friends, colleagues, people from his village, and our former students. Many of them had been fighters, also called patriots. It was easy to recognize them, as they all wore plastic sandals and most had "Afro" hairstyles. Women patriots wore pants, long or short — quite a surprise after our Peace Corps years when all women wore dresses. I was struck by the calm and dignified manner of the fighters. I recorded in my journal, "It seems that there is at least one patriot per family — brother, sister, cousin, in-law, etc. I'm meeting patriots all the time as part of families we knew."

I asked one of the patriots I met why he had joined the struggle. He responded, "I could not sit around with my parents when my friends and teachers went 'to the field,' so I joined in 5th grade." He spent seventeen years fighting to free Eritrea. In the field he found that the Eritrean People's Liberation Front — the main faction in the revolution — was well organized and cared for the people under their control. All Eritreans were patriots, he said, even if they didn't go to the field and fight. They were emotional patriots. "We fighters were more idealistic. Our cause was just." Disabled, he worked in Asmara at a center for disabled fighters.

TSEHAYE

I had gone to Asmara with handfuls of photos for people from Laurie's and my Peace Corps time. Ghebrecristos helped me find everybody in the pictures, including Tsehaye, now a lecturer in English at the University of Asmara. He said, "Mrs. Laurie, my English teacher, influenced me to study English, and now I am an English teacher at the University of Asmara." Tsehaye, one of the tallest students in Adi Teclesan, had a reserved cautiousness about him, always respectful and thoughtful.

One day during my visit Tsehaye and I took an old blue bus — an hour to go 25 miles — to Adi Teclesan, Laurie's and my first home. On the way, he pointed out the place where he narrowly escaped death by crawling underneath his Volkswagen beetle when he was caught in a gun battle. "See that small forest next to the road?" he asked. "I was stopped there by a group of Ethiopian soldiers. I was ordered to get out of my car. They pointed guns at me and asked me where I was going. I said that I was going to visit my parents in Teclesan. Suddenly, patriots started shooting at the Ethiopians. Bullets were everywhere, and I went under my car. I was very frightened. After the shooting stopped, the soldiers showed me the corpse of one of the patriot fighters to see my reaction. He was from Teclesan so I knew him, but I couldn't show any recognition or they might kill me." His ability to control his emotions had saved his life.

Observing the countryside from the bus, I noticed that there were almost no trees or vegetation. Where farm plots used to be only on flat bottom areas, they were terraced all the way up to the tops of hills. All of the villages had increased in size two to three times.

As the bus passed the house where we had lived, I blurted out, "Our first house is a wreck!" The paint was nearly gone, and the compound wall had been partially destroyed in a bombing by the Derg because it was suspected of being an office for the liberation movement. The three-room plastered stone house had been the most colorful cut stone building in the village — the plastered surface painted a bright turquoise, the unplastered stones and grout in the center were painted black and white — definitely gaudy. It had a corrugated metal roof and was one of the first "modern" houses in the village.

Laurie and her good friend, Mhret, in Adi Teclesan in 1969. Laurie and Wayne's daughter is named after Mhret.

The view from our two front doors took in fog rolling over the top of the escarpment to the east, the one school, the old slender-steepled Catholic church, a small forest of eucalyptus trees with the village well beyond it, the district court house, and the police station with the only telephone, which ran off a car battery and had to be cranked by hand. By early 1992, Adi Teclesan had a new well, a secondary school, and so many more houses that "ours" was barely visible from the road. The round Orthodox church was still carefully painted, although the three ostrich eggs attached to the points of the cross on top were missing.

Our first stop was lunch with Tsehaye's parents in their traditional house with rough-cut stone walls and a flat sod roof. It was large by Eritrean standards, some 8 yards by 16 yards — at least half the space taken up at night by their goats and cattle. In this house on Orthodox Christmas of 1965, we had our first ga'at tesmi, a very stiff porridge of wheat or barley flour formed into a volcano shape in a bowl with melted spiced rancid butter in the cone and sour milk like a moat around the outside of the volcano, and spiced red pepper sprinkled in the moat. We'd just had Christmas dinner with Ghebrecristos's family, stuffing ourselves with meat stew, vegetables and injera at their urging. So the ga'at tesmi felt like lead balls trying to make way in our stomachs.

Tsehaye's father was pleased to learn that Laurie and I had children, but he exclaimed in Tigrinya, "What, only two? How old is Laurie?" "Hamsa (50)," I replied. "She is too old to have any more. So, Wayne, you'll have to get another wife, then you can have more children." I didn't know how to explain that we were happy with only two.

She wanted to prepare a meal for us, but when we declined, she rummaged around and produced six eggs for me to take to Laurie in California. I almost cried.

As we went around the town to deliver photos we saw people who remembered Laurie and me. I was amazed, but Tsehaye pointed out that I still had a beard and glasses, so I really hadn't changed that much. We surprised our housekeeper, Ababa. She kissed me dozens of times on my cheeks and hands. I gave her copies of some photos which she kissed and kissed. Perhaps she would add them to those hanging on the wall of her one-room dirt-floor house along with photos of relatives' weddings, one of me and Laurie during our Peace Corps years, and one of her taken by me. She wanted to prepare a meal for us, but when we declined, she rummaged around and produced six eggs for me to take to Laurie in California. I almost cried.

I was hoping to find Bashai Keleta, my grandfather figure, but he had passed away. He was worldly-wise having served as an Italian soldier during World War II, and I had spent hours talking with him about the state of the world when I was a Peace Corps Volunteer.

Next stop was the elementary school, where I photographed the current teaching staff on the very steps where I'd photographed the staff we were part of twenty-six years earlier. What a difference! I found women in trousers, and both women and men with big Afro hair. I left copies of the original staff photo at the school. Before I left, the headmaster hauled me off to the library and proudly showed me an old set of the World Book Encyclopedia. Very little else was stacked on the nearly bare shelves. So, why was I being shown these? He explained, "The Derg burned English books or took them to Ethiopia. These books did not go. The janitor hid these in his house for 15 years." I took a closer look. Some of the books were from old Peace Corps collections, and the Encyclopedia set had been sent to the school by my librarian mother in 1966. I was delighted by these details from our past in Adi Teclesan.

... the Encyclopedia set had been sent to the school by my librarian mother in 1966.

GHEBRECRISTOS

Ghebrecristos also invited me to his village — Woki — that Laurie and I had visited several times during our Peace Corps years. A typical Orthodox Christian village, it lies on top of a rocky hill, right on the edge of the escarpment that falls 8,000 feet toward the Red Sea.

The well-maintained church towered over the houses. From it we could see the small patches of stony soil for growing wheat and barley, as well as the rocky hillsides where little children herded their goats, sheep, oxen and the ever present, always-braying donkeys. Ghebrecristos took me to see the clinic that was dedicated in July 1966 and still functioning with a couple of nurses. Sadly it was decrepit and dirty, yet I was glad to see it standing as it was the only concrete reminder of my Peace Corps activities — I had helped to obtain funding for the construction.

Next we went to the two-room house that Ghebrecristos built while we were teaching with him in Adi Teclesan. He told me that during a raid on Woki, the Derg soldiers took all of his 200 to 300 books, including some we had given him, put them with some furniture in the center of one of the rooms, and set fire to them, hoping to burn his house down. Ghebrecristos chuckled when he pointed to the ceiling still blackened from the fire. "Do you remember that you thought I was foolish to build the ceiling so high?" he asked. "That foolishness saved my house."

A week later, the Woki Development Committee presented me with a large plaque in appreciation for my help in establishing the clinic all those years ago. It's a metal map of Eritrea with the provinces named in Tigrinya and with the flags of the EPLF and of Eritrea under the United Nations mandate after World War II. With this gift, they were drawing us back to Eritrea.

BACK IN ASMARA

Ghebremicael and Tsehaye both invited me to their English classes, partly to show me off and partly to get a break from strict routines. What was I going to say for an hour? "Just say anything you like," they both said. "None of the students have heard native English speakers before."

In Ghebremicael's class at Ibrahim Sultan Secondary School (named after one of the founders of the liberation struggle) I told them about my family in California, and Laurie and my previous stay in Eritrea. Ghebremicael prompted me when I ran out of steam and tried to get his students to ask me questions. No one volunteered, so the school director ordered a student to ask a question. Straight out of geography class came, "How many square kilometers is California?" Tsehaye's university class was a little better, but I never heard them say a complete correct sentence.

Later I brought up this lack of English competency with Beraki Ghebreselassie, then the Minister of Education. He got right to the problem. "The Derg banned English from elementary and high schools. We have to catch up after 20 years because now it is the policy of our government to make English the language of schools, business and government. We do not have a curriculum. We do not have trained English teachers. We do not have textbooks." Then he asked me if I could find him an English curriculum development specialist who could volunteer for two to three months. "Coincidentally," I replied, "my wife Laurie is an English as a Second Language specialist." "Good!" exclaimed Beraki, "When can she come?" Laurie was being pulled back whether she knew it or not.

Farewell and Returning

On the last day before my return to California, there was a farewell party with beer and Eritrean hamburgers, and all our former students and colleagues Ghebrecristos could find, Ghebremicael, Mebrat, Tshaye, and Mebrahtom among them. It was quite a party, an emotional feast. For several hours we reminisced, told old jokes, took photographs. They all were saying how much they wanted me and Laurie to return and join them in building their new country. Their pervasive excitement and eagerness to establish and develop the country took hold of me. "In fact, excitement would be the one word that I would use to describe the whole country, a bubbling excitement," I wrote in my journal.

Wayne shows some children at the party photos from his and Laurie's Peace Corps time in Eritrea

Mulling over my enthusiasm for Eritrea's vision for development, its ideal of self-reliance, its efforts to unify its ethnic groups, and its policy of equal opportunity for women, I also wrote in my journal: "I often get overwhelmed by the need — so many areas of possibility — and I'm only one and not in a position of power or influence. I can't promise much, yet so much could be done, should be done. The Eritrean people are so deserving and the provisional government seems to be heading in the right direction on the road to creating a new nation. I wonder what could knock them off the track — lack of foreign support leading to impatience and then to anarchy? The one thing going for Eritrea is the spirit of the people — uplifting, full of hope, energetic, friendly, willing — some of the best qualities I've ever experienced and the best qualities for a society."

On departure day I wrote, "It is so, so, so easy to get caught up and absorbed by the deserving need of Eritreans. It becomes the focus of everything."

2011

I was so, so, so right. My enthusiasm was catching, and both Laurie and I turned much of our energy to Eritrea. At the invitation of the Minister of Education, Laurie spent the summers of 1993 and 1994 developing curriculum for English instruction. I returned in 1994 to work on establishing enCORPS, a program of Ethiopia & Eritrea RPCVs to bring former Volunteers back to their countries of service to share the knowledge and experience they had acquired since finishing their time in the Peace Corps. Laurie and I returned to Eritrea in early 1995 as independent volunteers and stayed for seven years. I worked with enCORPS and with a small business development partnership of Eritreans and Americans, then with the Pavoni Social Centre in technical education and humanitarian relief, and Laurie taught English at the University of Asmara and served as director of the Asmara International Community School.

We left Eritrea in 2002 after the border war with Ethiopia when the leadership became dictatorial and the economy closed in on itself. Regardless, we continue to correspond with our lifelong friends from our early Peace Corps days.

This article was written by Wayne in 1992.

Agordat

A Small, Remote Village

BY TOM CUTLER (AGORDAT 1963–1964)

I HAD GONE TO ETHIOPIA in 1962 with the first group of Peace Corps Volunteers assigned to the country, and was stationed in Addis Ababa where I taught 9th and 10th grade history to 150 students. It was a great year in the school, with hard-working students and fellow teachers, and on a personal

Tom, standing tall at right center, caroling with other Volunteers

level, with my three roommates. But toward the end of the school year, I began to think that this was not a real "Peace Corps Experience," living, as I was, in a large city, in a real 3 bedroom / 2 bath house with a cook and night watchman (using the term loosely), fraternizing with a large number of British, Swedish, and other expatriates, and singing Christmas carols for the Emperor. I asked Peace Corps Country Director Harris Wofford if I could be transferred to a small village somewhere out in the more rural part of the country. Soon I heard that one of the two Volunteers currently living in a remote village in Eritrea called Agordat was transferring to Massawa, and I was to replace him.

Happily the other Volunteer in Agordat, Tom Gallagher, was staying, and he became my mentor, translator (from and to the Arabic spoken there, as well as Tigrinya), my teacher of the local history and mores . . . and my good friend. We each taught four or five different courses to 7th and 8th graders — many of whom were in their high teens age-wise. I taught English, history, science, math and a bit of music. The kids were hard working, friendly and sometimes boisterous like most kids.

The Eritreans did not like being ruled by Ethiopia. There were major differences of language, religion, customs, and history. Once in a while, a student wouldn't appear at school for a day or three and it would be rumored that he had gone into the mountains to join the shifta — "insurgents" in today's parlance.

Tom Cutler on the left, and Tom Gallagher on the right with some of their 8th grade students — 1963

OVER THE CHRISTMAS HOLIDAYS, Tom and I, along with the four Peace Corps Volunteers stationed in the neighboring, larger town of Keren, hatched a plan to go camping. Unfortunately, poor Tom became sick the day before our scheduled departure, so the remaining five of us, Terry Moon, Terry O'Herron, Barbara Fountain and Linda Hughes and I, having borrowed a Peace Corps Land Rover and some camping gear, set out for the Red Sea north and east of Asmara.

Our first day out we passed through a missionary station and a small village and then wanted to head east to the beach. However, the track we took headed north and never turned east so we spent the day bumping along to the north until a flat tire stopped us. We put on the spare and pitched camp. We were ready to turn around and head back home the next morning.

Along the way we were treated to a drink of curdled milk cut with camel urine from two generous passing traders.

However when morning came we awoke with new energy and were determined to make it to our destination. Then after only going about a mile we had another flat. The tire patch kit was unusable, so Terry O. and I started to walk back to the little village we had passed the day before. We walked all the first day and some of the night before sleeping in the sand . . . then all the next day. Along the way we were treated to a drink of curdled milk cut with camel urine by two generous passing traders. We played charades with them and learned that there was a village — "our" village? — "just over the next hill."

We thanked the men for the drink and climbed over at least ten more hills, then lay down for a short snooze. It seemed just a few moments later that we awoke to see a pack of vultures circling maybe 20 feet above us looking for dinner . . . possibly us. We quickly got to our feet and climbed over another few hills until we saw, in the distance, a small village with campfires burning, and camels at rest. It was the most beautiful sight of my life . . . a scene like one on a Christmas card.

We must have been an odd sight limping into the village like a couple of lost Martians, but we were welcomed with great hospitality. We were fed and given cots to rest on, our feet were treated, and, luckily, we were introduced to the village head man who spoke some English and just happened to be making his once-a-month visit to the village. He graciously offered to take us back to the missionary station where we called a U.S. military Rest and Relaxation Station in Keren. They sent a large Land Rover out to pick up Terry and me, and then drove the sixty miles we had walked to pick up the other Volunteers — who were well and happy, darn it.

DURING THE LAST FEW MONTHS of our Peace Corps service, Tom and I had the idea to try to build a library for our school that would be funded by local villagers, and our parents and their friends back in the U.S. We thought we could get books donated from various libraries and organizations stateside.

What is incredible is that the plan actually came to fruition. We hit up all the village shop keepers and our relatives, bought building materials and hired a local builder. We invited fellow Volunteers Terry and Lois Shoemaker and Peace Corps staff member Gerry Faust and his wife, Marcia, to come down from Asmara to help build the thing (they knew what they were doing . . . Tom and I were good at mixing the cement).

As we had hoped, books were donated, and the year after we left Agordat the library opened for business. Evidently, the building still stands today, though it is now two classrooms — no longer a library. It's amazing what two young, naive kids can do if they haven't yet learned what "red tape" means.

EARLY JUNE OF 1964 brought the whole experience to a close. After a wonderful parting feast with our fellow teachers, Tom and I boarded a bus for Asmara, along with lots of local passengers and their chickens and other livestock, and both of us cried copiously for many miles . . . this time looking like lost and very unhappy Martians.

Tom and I boarded a bus for Asmara, along with lots of local passengers and their chickens and other livestock, and both of us cried copiously for many miles.

ABOUT SIX OR SEVEN YEARS ago my now long-time friend Tom came to visit me along with one of our students from Agordat and his family. Mohamed was his name. His wife had come to the U.S. on a nursing work permit. He said he remembered me, but when I asked him what, if any, specific knowledge he recalled learning from me, he paused, thought hard and said . . . "the song Row, Row, Row Your Boat."

Tom thinks he taught the students that, but I know I did.

MY PEACE CORPS EXPERIENCE was one of the highlights of my life.

Salaam, Salaam Alaykum and Cameloha

BY TOM GALLAGHER (AGORDAT 1962–1964)

MY FIRST VIEW OF AGORDAT was on a hot summer day in 1962. I was driven there by an officer of the U.S. Consulate in Asmara. He was going to Tessenei and agreed to drop another Volunteer and me off on his way. I was horrified when I saw Agordat's dusty streets and tukuls. My roommate and I decided to continue on to Tessenei with the man from the Consulate. We told ourselves that it was a chance to see another part of Eritrea, but in reality we were suffering the world's worst case of culture shock. We were scared to death and we clung to the man who was our last hope of contact with America. How did I get myself into this mess?

I GOT MYSELF INTO THIS MESS by joining the Peace Corps. I was 21, and had graduated from Monmouth College in New Jersey only five days earlier. It was the Peace Corps' first summer. My group, Ethiopia I, was the first to go through training in our nation's capital at Georgetown's excellent School of Foreign Service. It was the summer of '62, the best year of the Kennedy administration, and we were truly Camelot's kids.

Peace Corps put together a facebook of the more than 300 trainees in the group, and I was intimidated by my colleagues. Bill Tilney held the world's record for the 400 yard dash. Martha

Stonequist had played piano concerts in Vienna and Madrid. There were two Wiffenpoofs from Yale, and a graduate of Harvard Law School. Some of my colleagues were over 60 and had professional credentials that still amaze me. Paul Tsongas, who later became a Senator from Massachusetts and ran against Bill Clinton for the Democratic nomination in '92 was one of my fellow Volunteers. The Ethiopia Country Director, Harris Wofford, had held Martin Luther King's left hand at the bridge at Selma, and was generally credited with having gotten John Kennedy elected President. But under my picture in the facebook my bio read: "He has worked as a caddy, a valet parking attendant, and as a stock boy for Food Circus Incorporated." I was humiliated. Did they have to spell out "Food Circus Incorporated"?

Every liberal in Washington wanted to come and have his picture taken with us. Our speakers that summer included: Chief Justice Earl Warren, Senator Jay Rockefeller, the noted anthropologist Margaret Meade, and Supreme Court Justice William Douglas. We were seen off at a tea party in the Green Room of the White House hosted by JFK and Jackie, and were welcomed on our arrival in Addis Ababa by His Imperial Majesty Haile Selassie I, King of Kings, Elect of God, Conquering Lion of the Tribe of Judah and Emperor of Ethiopia — who was God to the Rastafarians. We sang the Etiopia Hoy (the national anthem) to him in Amharic, and he spoke to me in English, a language in which he was fluent, but rarely used because Emperors should not speak with accents.

At Georgetown we were trained in the Amharic language and told that we would all be assigned to cool towns in the mountains of the Christian country of Ethiopia. It was the first time

I learned that one should never trust what the government tells you. A week after meeting His Imperial Majesty, I was assigned to Agordat, an Arabic-speaking Muslim village in the Saharan lowlands near the Sudan border where the temperatures sometimes rose to 120 degrees Fahrenheit. I was born on Manhattan Island, grew up in a suburb of New York called Deal, New Jersey which is the richest town in the United States. (I hasten to note that my widowed, immigrant mother and I lived in the servants' quarters behind the garage, but we were surrounded by opulence.) My only trips away from home had been to Montreal and Philadelphia. I had never even seen a small town, and had no idea how to behave in one.

MY INSTINCT WAS TO RUN right back home to Jersey; but I couldn't afford the fare, so I started teaching in the Agordat middle school — a job for which I had absolutely no training at all. We were told to teach in English, but our students later admitted that they didn't understand a word we said for the first six months we were there. But they loved us anyway. Up to that point their educations had consisted of memorizing the Koran and multiplication tables with teachers who kept order by hitting them on the wrists with rulers. We laughed with them, taught them to sing songs about coming "from Alabama with a banjo on my knee," and tried to get them to think logically rather than to simply memorize. For the first time in their lives, school became fun.

(I should note that last year I met some of my former students in Jidda. One of them insisted on singing all the songs I taught him. So there we were in a fancy restaurant in Saudi Arabia with this crazy Eritrean singing "Row, row, row your boat." Thirty-five

One of them insisted on singing all the songs I taught him. So there we were in a fancy restaurant in Saudi Arabia with this crazy Eritrean singing "Row, row, row your boat."

years after leaving Eritrea when I was the Country Officer at the U.S. State Department for Ethiopia and Eritrea, I met most of the ministers and high ranking officials from both countries. The minute I told them I had been in the Peace Corps their faces turned into huge smiles. "Miss Johnson was my teacher. Did you know her?" they all asked; even though Miss Johnson had been a Volunteer ten years after I left the Peace Corps.)

When I arrived in Agordat, only one student from Eritrea's Western Province had ever gone as far as 9th grade, but because my Peace Corps group doubled the number of secondary school teachers in Ethiopia, new schools were built and forty-six of our students would go on to Keren's new high school. (I met several of them recently for the first time in many years, and was very impressed with their accomplishments. I met a civil servant, an ecologist, a surgeon and a man who reversed my steps and came to Seattle from Eritrea to teach Americans. They've come a long way.)

DURING THE THREE MONTHS of our Peace Corps training we Peace Corps trainees were never told that there was political dissent in Ethiopia. We firmly believed that all of the people there loved the Emperor who had brought them education and jet planes. Nobody told us about the four billion dollars he had stashed away in Swiss banks while his subjects starved. One day a small newspaper clipping was hung on a bulletin board at Georgetown which said that a small bomb had been set off by some sort of rebels in Ethiopia. There was no further explanation. We had no idea why anyone in Haile Selassie's paradise might be unhappy.

Upon arriving in Agordat, I was given a tour of the town by my dear, dear friend Sheik Hamid Mohammed el-Hadi who some of you may remember as the Education Officer for western Eritrea. At the Senior District Officers' building, Hamid showed us a few stones that he said had been put there in remembrance of a bomb that had been placed there. I remembered the article on the bulletin board at Georgetown and began peppering Hamid with questions. But he was no fool, and was not about to talk politics with a stranger. So I remained in ignorance for a while longer.

A month after my arrival in Agordat, a muffled "boom" went off while I was trying to teach a seventh grade history class. It was another bomb at the Senior District office building, and this time, for the first time, some people who called themselves "the Eritrean Liberation Front" took credit for the event. It was the first time that the ELF announced its existence; previously they were merely referred to as shifta; so I claim to have heard the first shot of the longest war of the 20th century. Most Americans have never even heard of Eritrea, or its wars; but they have remained a part of my life ever since that day.

As Sheik Hamid and other local people came to trust me, I learned why people were throwing bombs. I became aware of the discrimination that Eritreans faced and as my students slipped away, one-by-one, to join the guerillas in the hills, I realized that I had joined the Peace Corps, but found myself in the middle of a war.

One day our school was buzzed by three U.S. manufactured F-85s flying at an altitude of 80 feet. It was His Imperial Majesty's way of telling us to behave. Few people in Agordat had ever even seen an airplane, and the noise was terrifying. People in the market panicked, and all of the students jumped out of classroom windows in terror — except for my 6th grade class which followed their teacher's example and hit the floor. When we got up, the kids were laughing and I knew that I was the butt of the joke. "What's so funny," I asked; but they were too scared to tell me until a brave Somali boy, Mohammed Ali Elmi, stood up very rigidly, closed his eyes, and said: "But Sir, we have never seen a white man become whiter before."

"But Sir, we have never seen a white man become whiter before."

FOR OUR SECOND CHRISTMAS IN ERITREA the Volunteers who were stationed in Keren and my roommate and I decided to go as far away from western civilization as we could, so we borrowed a Jeep from the Peace Corps and headed for the Red Sea. Not to Massawa — we were Peace Corps Volunteers. We went to the bush. We decided to go swimming on a beach due east of Nakfa, 50 miles north of Massawa. Unfortunately, I got sick on Christmas Eve and decided that I was too weak to undertake a long, hard trip; so I returned to Agordat by bus to spend my Christmas all alone and very depressed.

At about noon on Christmas Day our cook, Mohammed, came running in speaking rapidly in Arabic urging me to go with him to the market to see a "sura" of some shifta. I understood the word "sura" to mean "picture." But I learned that day that it can mean any framed object. I went out to the village square in front of our house where I noticed that the people were very quiet, and all of them had their eyes fixed on me. Suddenly I looked to my right and saw the "sura." In fact it was a gibbet that framed the suspended body of a man who had died for

It was a gibbet that framed the suspended body of a man who had died for his country, Eritrea.

his country, Eritrea. His body had nearly been cut in half by automatic weapon fire. It was my first view of the insides of a human body. The government hung him publicly as an example to others who might think of revolution. I was horrified — and turned white all over again. I went into the local general store which was run by a wonderful Eritrean/Cypriot "caffe-latte" named Eftemios Fangarides who knew that December 25 was an American holiday. He looked at me as I entered his store, pointed to the unfortunate hero and said "This is our Christmas tree." Subsequently, the government hung seven other men in front of my house. These events were intended to intimidate the Eritreans; but, in fact, they served only to piss off the Eritrean populations and send more of them into the hills to fight.

LEST I SOUND TOO GLUM about my experience, I should note that there were moments of great fun in Agordat. One day, the American publisher, Golden Books, sent us a collection of their publications. Golden Books were written for very bright 4th graders who were asking intelligent questions about geology, archeology, and astrophysics among other things. They were perfect for our kids who were very bright teenagers, but who had about a 4th grade level of English comprehension. Up to that point the only books we had were 2nd grade readers donated by the good people of Darien, Connecticut. They were about Dick and Jane and their dog Spot. You can imagine how the Muslims in our all-boys school reacted to Americans playing with girls and dogs! These new books were a God-send, but we had no library to put them in.

My roommate, Tom Cutler, and I sat down with two Eritrean teachers to discuss how we might make the books available to the students. The Eritreans were all for building a tukul for a new library on our small campus. I was cynical. "Where will we get the money?" There had never been a community fund-raising event in our little town, and anyway, Ethiopia was, and remains, the poorest country in the world. My colleagues argued that we could ask the rich Italian farmers and Arab merchants in town for donations, and try to do the construction ourselves — even though none of the four of us knew how to hammer a nail.

My mother's employer had sent me a $100 Christmas gift with a card instructing me to "do something nice for your kids." I was annoyed because I wanted the money for myself, but I felt obliged to obey her wishes. I told the Eritrean teachers that I had $100, and would use it to match anything that we could raise in town. We wrote to the Italians and the Arabs, and they came through with sizeable donations. We went door-to-door through the market collecting whatever pennies the merchants could afford. To the great glee of my students, in broad daylight I walked into every whorehouse in town to ask the ladies for money rather than to give them some. They were so proud that the American teacher spoke to them in public, and asked them to be a part of a community project that they put their hands into their cleavages and pulled out dollar bills.

In the end we raised over $1,000 and all sorts of donations of bricks and mortar.

In the end we raised over $1,000 and all sorts of donations of bricks and mortar. Local carpenters and masons volunteered their time. Fellow PCVs from all over Eritrea came on weekends to help us complete our project. In the end, the school got two new classrooms, the Golden Books got their library, and I got a great lesson in how effective Eritreans can be in developing their communities.

SHORTLY AFTER THE LIBRARY WAS BUILT, one of the students cut out the picture of Haile Selassie from a beautiful set of Encyclopedia Americana that the Peace Corps had donated to the school. I was furious. Like everyone else in Agordat, I had learned to hate the Emperor who so abused what had now become "my people" in Eritrea; but defacing the most beautiful book in town seemed like a bad way to make a revolution against HIM. My fellow Eritrean teachers urged me to stifle my anger and let it go, but I roared into every classroom in the middle school to berate the boys and to demand an apology from the perpetrator.

We had a new student in the eighth grade at the time who was half-Amhara, half-Eritrean. His father was a military officer stationed at the army base in Agordat. The boy told his father about the incident, who told Captain Habtemariam, the number two police officer in Agordat. The Captain, who as an Eritrean needed to prove his loyalty to the Emperor, summoned the Headmaster — Saleh Karar, the Assistant Headmaster — the wonderful Osman Omrun, and the two Peace Corps teachers to his office where he spent fifteen minutes denouncing us and threatening to arrest all the teachers, all the students and all of their fathers until he got a confession from the evil student who had done the deed. I was scared witless and was sure I would be run out of the Peace Corps for dabbling in local politics; but Saleh, Osman and my roommate were too frightened to speak; so it was left to me to respond. I was sitting at Captain Haptemariam's desk, so he could see my head and torso, but not my legs. I gave him a reasoned response confirming that I shared his anger at the destruction of property; but that this was ultimately the silly act of a teen-aged boy not the act of a serious revolutionary. My colleagues later told me that while my head and torso seemed calm, my legs, which Captain Haptemariam could not see, were shaking like leaves in a tornado. Fortunately, the day after this incident Captain Habtemariam's boss returned to town and cancelled the Captain's investigation of teenaged revolutionaries. Several years later I met the student who had squealed on us at a restaurant in Addis Ababa. By that time he had changed his politics so dramatically that I had to tell him to stop talking about his love for the Eritrean revolution lest he end up in Addis' "carceli."

GOING BACK TO the political struggles for a moment: I never thought the Eritreans could win. The odds were stacked against them. Ethiopia was much bigger. It received arms and training from all the major powers, while the Eritreans had no foreign allies. Nonetheless, I supported the revolution and to this day consider myself to be the first American supporter of Eritrean freedom.

Before the war was over, my dear friend and fellow Agordat teacher, Mohamoud Mohammed Saleh, was running an underground Ministry of Education that brought about nearly 100 per cent literacy, operated universities, and ran classes for Ethiopian prisoners of war. The Eritrean revolutionaries built a five mile long hospital in caves which had operating rooms of such high quality that in later years I attended a dinner in San Francisco that opened a program through which the University of California brought Eritrean doctors from that cave to teach the Californian medical students how to handle gunshot wounds in emergency rooms. And the Eritreans accomplished all that without a nickel of foreign aid.

The Peace Corps frequently thought about taking us out of harm's way in Agordat; but they let us finish our tours. Our directors later told me that they allowed me to stay there because they had heard that I was smart enough never to discuss politics in public. I believed strongly that the Peace Corps was not sent to other countries to interfere in local politics, so I controlled my emotions and did a lot more listening than talking. But there were no rules against teaching my students about Thomas Jefferson, or about Lawrence of Arabia's leadership of an Arab revolt against the Turkish Empire, or about my family's involvement with the 800-year-long Irish struggle for freedom. They got the message. In retrospect, I'm not sure that I did any of those young heroes a favor by telling them about Jefferson, Lawrence and the IRA. Sometimes I have nightmares about inspiring them to die for their country. But most of the time I think that I did the best I could.

I sure am glad [Peace Corps] let me stay my full two years in Agordat.

Nowadays the Peace Corps is a lot more careful about placing Volunteers in war zones; but I sure am glad they let me stay my full two years in Agordat.

IN 1997 MY PEACE CORPS ROOMMATE Tom and I returned together to Agordat — 34 years after we had left, and six years after Eritrea won its independence from Ethiopia. When we first came there in 1962 there were only 12 students in the 8th grade, our highest class. In 1997 there were 1,100 students in the regional high school. The Eritrean economy was growing at seven per cent a year. Agordat had a functioning hospital, and the road from Asmara was being paved all the way across western Eritrea. The town which had scared me so in 1962 now seemed beautiful to me.

I took a hike to the Turkish fort on a small hill overlooking Agordat. From there I could see the extinct volcanoes that ringed the area, and the "bannarie" farms on the banks of the Barka with their thick groves of dom palms. The mosque still seemed like the most beautiful one in the world to me, and the tukuls seemed homey. The desert really does have a majestic beauty.

But sadly, there was not one person left in town who remembered us. The Ethiopian army killed nearly 500 people in the Agordat market on one awful day during the war. Most of my kids joined the revolution, and many died as heroes for their country. The rest had gone into exile in Sudan, Saudi Arabia, Qatar and Sweden. One made it to Maryland and another to Virginia. Almost everyone in town was under 34-years old, and could not possibly have known us. Even the predominant language had changed from Arabic to Tigrinya. But the two-room addition to the school which we built was still standing — albeit used only as a storeroom for the much bigger new school.

Much to my dismay, about a month after my 1997 visit, Eritrea and Ethiopia again went to war. The fighting started, not surprisingly, about 30 miles from Agordat. The Peace Corps was forced to pull out the one Volunteer in the town, Maria Said, on very short notice. When she and I had dinner in Washington after her return, she told me of how sad she was that she never even had a chance to say "good-bye" to many of her students and friends.

I was Country Officer for Eritrea and Ethiopia at the State Department on the day the two countries went back to fighting. A fellow Peace Corps Volunteer and I worked our asses off to stop that carnage, and we came very close to success. But we failed, and 100,000 people died. I still don't know why, and the nightmares continue.

Eritrea gave me the best two years of my life for which I will be eternally grateful. It also gave me the best friends I've ever had. I'm still in touch with my refugee students in Jidda, Qatar and Maryland, and with Sheik Hamid who lives in Sudan. I met him and Ostaz (teacher) Osman Omrun in Jidda last year. They are still strikingly handsome and they've survived. Like this group, my Peace Corps group has had about 20 reunions, and I hope we live long enough to have 20 more. We've stayed in touch for nearly half-a-century.

WHEN TOM AND I LEFT AGORDAT, our kids came out to the bus station to wave good-bye. The bus drivers always honked their horn as they put their foot on the gas. As the kids' hands rose to wave their last farewell in response to that horn, my roommate and I started to sob. We cried for the next half-hour while 80 fellow passengers sat in amazed silence staring at the strange behavior of American men.

Thank you all for giving an old man a chance to remember his youth and the great love he has for Eritrea and its people. Yukunyele.

Eritrea gave me the best two years of my life for which I will be eternally grateful.

Asmara

An Experience Not Easily Found

BY MARIANNE ARIEUX (ASMARA 1965–1967)

A SMALL GROUP OF 21 Peace Corps Volunteers arrived in Ethiopia on May 19, 1965. We were the fifth group of Peace Corps Volunteers to come to Ethiopia, but the first that was all women.

Our assignment was focused on health rather than education. We were registered nurses, several allied health professionals, health educators and one medical records librarian, and were assigned to various health care posts in villages and cities around the country. I had asked to be sent to a remote area, wishing to experience the country as unfettered by modernity as possible. That did not happen, and I was posted to Asmara, the second largest city in Ethiopia.

SOME DAYS AFTER OUR ARRIVAL those of us not assigned to the capitol boarded a bus for a 3-day trip on the winding and precipitous mountain road stretching from Addis Ababa to Asmara. While I was mostly enthralled with this country, the strange smells wafting from the flora, the century-old farming implements, and the poverty, I recall a hint of sadness as the bus stopped overnight in different towns to discharge another one or two of us. We were no longer the group we were when we arrived on the UCLA campus in February. Mekele in Tigre

Province was the last stop before heading toward the final destination, Asmara, Eritrea with just five of us left. At that time, Eritrea was a province of Ethiopia.

I was one of the registered nurses in the group, and was assigned to teach at Itegue Menen Dresser School in Asmara. I was also to assist Alganesh Kidane, an Eritrean registered nurse who was the head teacher and in charge of education at the school. Charlotte Lockner, a medical records librarian was also assigned to the school. Of the three other Volunteers, the two x-ray technicians were assigned to the hospital and the health educator, to a local school.

ALGANESH KIDANE WAS MY FIRST and most important connection to the country and remained so throughout my stay. She was an extraordinary person — a slip of a woman with an unvarying playful sense of humor. She was committed to good teaching and to our students' success — recognizing without making explicit the social justice implications played out in the education of young people as dressers.

My assignment to co-teach with Alganesh turned out to be a large part of the reason why my stay in Asmara was so wonderful. The school prospered. She was always a pleasure to be with as well as strikingly good at overcoming obstacles that arose in the course of making the dresser school a success. Her commitment to her country, to nursing and the joy which she brought to this work daily made her delightful. I admired her deeply and she returned that — although we never talked about it, it was simply present. I was invited to her home, and was brought along to social events with her and with other nurses.

Alganesh Kidane was my most important and immediate connection to the country initially and throughout my stay there.

Our "assigned relationship" became a deep connection, one that has become a treasured memory, a rich and special experience — one not easily found.

ALTHOUGH I HAD HOPED to be assigned to a very remote place, Asmara turned out to be the perfect assignment for me as I fell deeply in love with all aspects of the country that touched me — the work, the companionship of Alganesh, and the other nurses, the city and the culture from micro to macro that was so different from my own, and all the people I met from the Israeli doctor directing the hospital to the folks in Danakil villages.

Asmara was a hodgepodge perfectly suited to a person yearning for multiple diverse experiences like myself. It was deeply African with Mid Eastern spice, tinged with leftover tastes of Italian colonized culture.

Whatever had been the feelings of the Eritreans about being an Italian colony, by the time I arrived in Eritrea the major political pulse of the city was a growing dissatisfaction with having been made part of Ethiopia as a result of Haile Selassie's negotiation with the United Nations in his attempt to rid the country of the Italian military invaders.

Upon arriving in Asmara we quickly discovered we should not speak the language taught us during Peace Corps training at UCLA earlier in the year — Ethiopia's national language, Amharic. I quickly learned it would be an affront to speak Amharic in Eritrea since Ethiopia was considered an enemy. While Eritreans were schooled in Amharic, Tigrinya was their native language. The Peace Corps, recognizing the issue, rushed to hire us a Tigrinya tutor. It was difficult enough to teach in a language — English — that was the 3rd or 4th language for my students, but then to converse with them in a language of their current oppressors — that certainly was not the Peace Corps way, which was always to honor the country, to be as much a part of the community as possible, and hence give no offense.

THE HEALTH CARE SYSTEM in Ethiopia at the time seemed a brilliant plan for a developing country with scant medical personnel. There was a dearth of professionals such as doctors and medical educators. At Itegue Menen Hospital, the director was an Israeli physician and most of the doctors were Italian. While I was there the first Ethiopian doctors began to arrive from resident training in foreign schools. The nurses in positions of authority who ran the local nursing school had access to training at the American University of Beirut, and seemed to have an elite standing in the community. Like nurses everywhere, they were charged to carry out the doctors' orders.

Beyond the doors of the hospital the health care system of Ethiopia, which had been designed and implemented by the World Health Organization in concert with Ethiopian nationals, was a masterful innovation that addressed the health care needs of the country. Having too few health care personnel, a 3-pronged hierarchical system was devised to meet the health care needs in the mostly rural and very poor country. The few hospitals in the largest cities provided the most extensive medical care staffed with doctors, nurses and allied health professionals. These were supplemented by health care clinics in sizable towns manned by fewer medical personnel who were able to treat most medical health conditions not requiring major surgery. These in turn were supplemented by health stations (what might be likened to first aid stations) in the most rural, least populated areas. These latter were to be manned by dressers, hence the Itegue Menen Dresser School. Using the three-step design, medical care could be provided as efficiently and effectively as possible. I thought it a brilliant design for a country moving into the 20th Century, a model for developing nations with similar needs.

Dressers were comparable to licensed practical nurses in the U.S. except they did more — suturing up wounds, and delivering babies, but knew less theory. We learned that the name "dresser" arose from the medical personnel in the battlefields who literally "dressed" wounds. Opened in 1965, Itegue Menen Dresser School had a year-long program with exams required for entry. The graduates — young women and men — would be able to make a decent living, and get respect in their communities, although they might have to spend some time in a very rural area. Dressers, being the health care professionals on the lowest rung, had no choice.

IT WAS WITH THE KNOWLEDGE of the current Ethiopian/ WHO health care plan, the 3-month Peace Corps public health training, and my own experience as a diploma registered nurse from a 36-month program at Charity Hospital in New Orleans followed by six months of practice, that I became a teacher of nursing, and to a lesser degree, of English. I did not know it at the time, but my experience in Eritrea would herald what would become a life's career.

My experience at Charity Hospital turned out to be both a good and not-such-good preparation for teaching Ethiopian dressers.

Charity Hospital was flanked on either side by two large medical schools — Tulane and Louisiana State University. Nurses and nursing students were limited to procedures not required for doctors in training. Minimal assistance in deliveries was restricted as interns' and residents' needs for experience took precedence over ours. Charity Hospital was a focal point for a myriad of diseases not typical in most United States health care facilities. In addition to treating only the poor, who arrived with minimal access to prior medical care, the campus of Charity Hospital included a building for infectious diseases only, a fully functioning TB sanitarium, and a complete floor for mental illness. A leper sanitarium was in a nearby town, and the VA hospital was just next door. This meant that not much of what I observed health and illness wise in Ethiopia was new to me, but I knew neither how to suture nor how to deliver a baby, skills needed by dressers. Fortunately Alganesh Kidane was a master of these practices. As a result I taught more of the basic sciences while she instructed in the clinical nursing skills needed for dressers that were beyond my repertoire.

Classes proceeded at the Dresser School with the typical bumps amid successes. The germ theory of disease was not particularly well received although students had to accept it; and the idea of using a needle only once (no disposables) was an alien concept in spite of Alganesh's insistent repetitions and the threat that a student could fail the program due to improper practice.

During my two years in Asmara, the school graduated one class and welcomed in another. The first class had 44 students, and the second was even larger. In addition to teaching basic sciences and nursing skills, I also spent a lot of time helping my students

Marianne and her students on a field trip to a health care clinic

become more proficient in English as this was the language of medicine and of their education, although not of interaction with their patients. I enjoyed the classroom teaching as well as that in the units of the hospital, and on field trips. I did wonder a bit about how these youngsters could be expected to do so much, and how they would do if they were assigned to remote posts because most of them came from areas surrounding Asmara.

A PARTICULAR DELIGHT of my experience was my interaction with my peers. I became as close as one can be in such a situation with Alganesh. With her and in the company of other nurses there was always humor and good will. I felt very accepted and enjoyed being in their company. I became friendly with another nurse who was the daughter of the head of the province. She had a bachelor's degree in nursing and was the director of the Asmara Nursing School. She was married while I was there and I had the pleasure to be invited to the wedding. As her father was so prominent, it was an elaborate celebration, lasting days, that included both small family events and large public gatherings. These were lovely and gracious affairs reflecting the majority of Eritreans I met while there.

OTHER CULTURAL PRACTICES were equally pleasing as well as consonant to my way of being. I very much recall the shift from temporal ordering of actions so dominant in the States to the practice of putting human interaction first. I thought it delightful that one would be expected to greet and speak for some time with a friend, even if it meant being a bit late for work — as opposed to uttering a quick "fine" to the greeting of "how are you," the deplorable but very common practice in the U.S. It was not that time did not count in Eritrea and Ethiopia — it did; it just did not dominate. The nurses waiting for the next shift to arrive would not become upset at unexpected lateness by their replacements, since they too lived under similar rituals and expectations. I noticed for years after I had left Eritrea that my own natural time was about a half hour later than scheduled. It did not make my life easy for quite some time, but eventually I became Americanized again with time marking my actions.

THERE IS OF COURSE MUCH MORE to write about — the beauty of the country, the gloriousness of Asmara with its Italianate architecture influenced by the Eritrean life-style.

In addition, there was my sadness in leaving, my longing to return not so much for the geography as to recapture the spirit of Africa as manifested in Eritrean living, and most of all my concerns about upheavals to the lives of the people that would be caused by a the long war with Ethiopia.

All that is for another day, but there is one experience that I think is singular to my stay as a Peace Corps Volunteer in Eritrea.

SOMETIME IN THE SUMMER Of 1966, the doctors of the U.S. Army who were stationed at Kagnew Station, the U.S. military base, decided that they wanted to see the illnesses that were native to the country as evidenced in rural communities. I am guessing the visits were also meant to be a show of good will.

Many of the American doctors had trained at urban northern universities and hospitals in the U.S. where some of the diseases that I had previously observed at Charity Hospital were nonexistent. It was decided that they would travel to several remote villages on a medical safari using Army equipment, supplies and vehicles, to provide care — I was fortunate enough to be invited to accompany this group.

The villages that we visited were quite isolated though not far by automobile from towns the size of Keren, and were without any medical care other than that practiced by traditional "hakim" (doctors). We went to two villages. Unfortunately I do not recall the names of these places. If my memory serves me well, and it has been a long time, I recall that one village, the second, was in the Danakil desert or made up of Danakil warriors. I found these forays wonderful from a health perspective, and instructive of the health care needs in the remote places. It certainly would have been a different Peace Corps experience for me to have been posted in a village such as these, but not as diverse as the one I had as a teacher of dresser students in Asmara.

The villagers welcomed this convoy of people who did not look like them or speak their language. They were completely open to being examined, and they appreciated the treatment they received from the members of our team. I shall always remember this incomparable experience.

The greeting at one of the remote villages the medical team visited

I TRIED TO PROLONG MY STAY in Ethiopia, but it was impossible to secure a job, and my Peace Corps replacement was already scheduled to arrive. One of my fellow PCVs and I planned to take our travel money and instead of flying directly home, go overland through the Mideast. We left Asmara by bus for Tessenei on the border of the Sudan, and I have never had a chance to go back.

A FINAL NOTE: Alganesh Kidane, according to a recent web search, is now the Secretary General of the Red Cross in Eritrea. We were in brief email contact several years ago, but were not able to reunite, our separate lives having prevailed.

A Reminiscence

BY MIKE BANISTER (ASMARA 1973–1974)

WE ARRIVED IN ASMARA right around Cheryl's birthday in July of 1973. We were transferring there for our second year of our Peace Corps service. We flew by jet from Addis Ababa carrying everything we owned with us. Cheryl, who was pregnant, had been relentlessly sick, hardly able to stand up, and was fresh out of one hospital and bound for another. God only knows what it was that made Cheryl sick, but whatever it was, it stayed with her for ten long, hectic, miserable days.

In Addis Ababa the doctors at the hospital couldn't cure her, and the Peace Corps staff was becoming very worried. The first few days of the sickness the two Peace Corps nurses came to our room at the Itegue Hotel, and gazed down at poor Cheryl as she retched up noise and nausea pills. When it didn't stop after a few days, Peace Corps decided it was time for us to try the American military doctors at Asmara's Kagnew Station. At something like 5 a.m. the next day, a Peace Corps driver with a Volkswagen bus picked us up and deposited us at the airport.

One hour later we were touching down at the Asmara airport. We had exactly nowhere to go, no connections other than the Army/Navy base. Because of my inability to dial the correct sequence of numbers, I was unable to contact Kagnew and order up either an ambulance or a base taxi. So, for five Ethiopian dollars, a very sympathetic Eritrean cab driver piled his Alfa Romeo high with our luggage, guitar, household goods and all, and took us to a hotel in downtown Asmara. Only there at the hotel did I figure out how to use the phone; a half-hour later a blue Volkswagen bus driven by a Kagnew-ized Eritrean named Berhane picked us up, along with our belongings, and sped out to the base guest house — all for a thin American dime.

First the good news: We were extremely lucky in that there was a room available at the guest house. What luxury! Real American beds with box springs and mattresses, American furniture and American bathrooms down the hall. Now the bad news: In a week's time we would have to give up the room for a few days. The problem — where could we go for those few days before we could return to the nearness, convenience and safety of the guest house?

Well, before the problem became urgent, Cheryl was seen by an American Navy doctor named Stanley Bodner, a nice young man from New Jersey. He was fascinated at having the chance to talk to Peace Corps Volunteers who had spent time out in remote southwest Ethiopia. His interest in Cheryl's sickness seemed only secondary. He didn't think it was serious, and he certainly didn't think it merited hospitalization.

I was so frustrated and scared by the continuing deterioration of Cheryl's condition that I was ready to do anything to get her into the hospital. I went to Stanley's office the next morning and told him of the "blood" I saw in her vomit. She was admitted without further hassle. Stanley put her on IV feedings, and her condition began to improve rapidly. In another day or so,

Cheryl was completely better. There was absolutely no inkling of what the little bugger was that had waylaid my lover.

Stanley being the inquisitive, concerned person that he was — and is, found out about our housing dilemma vis-à-vis having to move out of the guest house for a few days, and invited us to stay in his home in the interim. That was the beginning of our long and warm friendship with Stanley.

AFTER BEING READMITTED to the Kagnew guest house a couple of days later, an Ethiopian Peace Corps staff person dropped in on us. He was in the area and had been asked to check on us, and it was he who was instrumental in helping us get settled.

Here is how that came about. He happened to be good friends with a certain Asmara nobleman who held the aristocratic rank of "Blatiengheta." He was a retired Eritrean gentleman named Ephrem Teklemariam. He used to be Haile Selassie's ambassador to Germany, and also was the Ethiopian delegate at the founding of the United Nations in San Francisco in 1945. Blatiengheta Ephrem, it just so happened, had a small villa for rent in the "Ghezabanda" (probably a corruption of the Italian term "casabanda") neighborhood of Asmara.

That very afternoon the Peace Corps staff person took us to the home of the Blatiengheta and his wife and introduced us to them. What an elegant domicile they had! So many refined European touches; the living room was distinctly German in atmosphere. After much small talk about travel and the world situation, we finally got around to discussing the rental of his villa, which happened to be only halfway down the block. As the rent was reasonable (compared to what we had been paying the year before in the coffee-rich Mettu, provincial capital of Illubabor in southwestern Ethiopia), we leased the place for the school year.

The view from the living room window

Our house was a single-story affair surrounded by a high wall and locking gate. The house and compound resembled many others in our neighborhood. It had two bedrooms with a bathroom between them, a kitchen, a dining room and a living room. It had Italian tile floors throughout. The living room had a large picture window with a stunning view of Asmara and our backyard.

Cheryl and I luxuriated in our new home during the remaining weeks before the birth of our baby, and before the start of the new school year. Peace Corps friends James and Marie Tarrant stayed with us for two weeks that summer. What fine times we had with those two warm, lovable people! We were also visited occasionally by other Peace Corps Volunteers passing through Asmara. Our non-PC friends were primarily Navy Dr. Stanley Bodner and Army Sgt. Mike Hoffman. Hoffman was our neighbor, and was a photographer doing "geologic mapping" for the Army and the Ethiopian government. We suspected he was really helping the government do counter-insurgency surveillance. Mike lived in the bottom half of a large house next door, with beautiful Moorish arches and large rooms. He kept two dogs (one was pregnant) and a large land tortoise that ate lettuce and flowers. It was Mike who told us that our house had formerly been rented by two Army guys who used it as a "friendship house," arranging romantic liaisons between soldiers and Eritrean ladies.

There were so many people and things to get to know in Asmara. By chance, or Providence, our need for a maid/baby-sitter coincided with the need of some friends who wished to find a new family for their maid, Tsehaitu, because they would soon be leaving Asmara. Tsehaitu turned out to be great, even though she spoke hardly a word of English or Amharic, being from a village outside Asmara. She did, however, speak some Italian, since she had worked for Italian families in the past. She worked for us five days a week, from about 8 a.m. until about 2 p.m. At times we asked her to stay later to help us prepare for a party. Occasionally she slept over when we wanted to go out and needed her to watch "Gianni." We paid her about $20 U.S. per month, plus all the empty bottles, jars, old clothes, etc. for which we had no use. These items she sold in the market. Her salary working for us was about twice what Ethiopians paid servants, and her workdays were short and easy.

WE WERE FAIRLY WELL SETTLED into our house when the time came for Cheryl to deliver herself of "Shorty." We had no scenario planned, except for a vague idea of calling the base taxi for a ride to the hospital when the time came. But good-neighbor Mike had volunteered to drive us to the hospital in his Land Rover. Long about mid-day on August 26, 1973, Cheryl calmly informed me that she had been experiencing periodic but irregular contractions since the previous evening. (We had attended a very nice party at Mike's that evening, and Cheryl kept her secret nicely.) Now she was beginning to feel the contractions more frequently and more regularly. James and Marie were still visiting with us, and they accompanied us in Mike's Land Rover over to the Kagnew hospital.

Dr. Donaldson said to relax, the birth wouldn't happen until around dawn, and promptly left to do his rounds, this being around 11 p.m. Around 1 a.m. Cheryl's contractions were occurring with enough frequency to warrant Donaldson's return. He got there around 2 a.m. and told me to get my gown, mask and hat on, and come with him, Cheryl and a nurse into the delivery room. After about an hour of labor, at 3:09 a.m. (not 3:10 as the birth certificate says) on August 27, 1973, a male child was born in the "land of burnt faces." During delivery I was trying to be both helpful and to get some good pictures. Besides some massage and hand-holding and morale encouragement, there wasn't much that I could do. Cheryl did it all beautifully.

For the next two days, Cheryl and the baby stayed at the hospital. Since we had been consistently unable to imagine a name for a baby boy (but had several possibilities for a girl), we planned to think of a name for him after Cheryl left the hospital. The hospital authorities thought differently, though, and suggested that we come up with a name in return for a swift exit from the hospital. Cheryl was fond of "Chris," after her mother, and I sort of thought the baby looked like my uncle John ("John" is also one of my favorite names). The name "John Christopher" also appealed to me, because it reminded me of John the Baptist, "bearing" the name of Christ the way Saint Christopher was supposed to have borne Christ Himself. Cheryl and John

Christopher Armstrong Banister left the hospital on the third day after his birth.

Tsehaitu began working for us immediately and quickly became attached to "J.C." as we called him for short. When our school started up, Tsehaitu entertained J.C. and cared for him for three

The view out the classroom window

hours or so every morning while Cheryl was teaching. Our school, the Asmara Junior Secondary School, located at the eastern edge of the city, near the escarpment which drops 8,200 feet to the Red Sea, was on split session. We taught the seventh and eighth graders from 8:30 a.m. to 1 p.m. — the ninth graders came in the afternoon. Cheryl talked the director into only scheduling her for the first three periods so she could be home by 11:30.

For the next couple of months we learned new ways to enjoy a city, ways involving packing a kid around on one's back or in one's arms. Riding a bus through the city with J.C., or riding one down the mountain and across the Danakil Depression to the port city of Massawa, brought us into contact with the Eritrean people (especially the women) in ways completely new. J.C. was such a flirt: We would be sitting there with him leaning against our shoulders facing the seat behind us, when pretty soon we would hear a little embarrassed laughter coming from some ladies behind us. J.C. would be putting on his best flirting grin. Out on the street we would often be taken to task in Tigrinya or Italian for not covering him up enough.

The Eritreans considered the sun and the wind to be dangerous for babies.

WE HAD SOME PETS BY THIS TIME, some domestic and some not so domestic. Right off we inherited the last of the litter of the German Shepherds pups belonging to Mike Hoffman's formerly pregnant dog. We named our new dog "Patty" and let her have full run of both yards, but she never came in the house. Tsehaitu never touched her or had anything to do with her.

Then we found two miserable little kittens at the fenced end of our block. They were covered with scabs and crud. It looked like they were going to die for sure. I was never so upset by an animal's condition as I was by theirs, so I decided to give the kittens a bite to eat. I was pretty sure they weren't long for this world and I wouldn't be feeding them for long. I was wrong. Day by day they looked better and better. We washed the crud off them and cleaned their eyes, and their scabs disappeared. They began purring when we touched them or even came near them. Patty tolerated them. Tsehaitu was a bit friendlier to them than to Patty. We named them "Anti" and "Ante," meaning "you" feminine and "you" masculine in Tigrinya. They looked like they were brother and sister.

A few months later I heard a terrible shouting and running-about next door. The landlord's servant and a friend had treed some animal in the cedar tree growing next to the wall dividing our yard from Mike's yard. The two Eritrean men were throwing rocks at whatever they had treed. All of a sudden a young baboon jumped down out of the tree and landed on the roof of our little outbuilding. The baboon then jumped into our backyard, scaring Patty half to death. The two tormenting men made like they were going to hop over the wall and pursue the baboon (which was an adolescent female), but I stopped them and said the baboon could stay in our yard and I didn't want them throwing rocks at her.

Every day we would see the baboon roaming the cliff edge and back wall of our yard, and she stripped all the figs and peaches off the trees in both Mike's and our yards. I tried to get close to her, but not a chance. After about two weeks of sporadic visits by her, she disappeared. We heard that she had escaped from some nearby factory yard where she was a "pet." I don't know what happened to her. I hope she made it out of town; not too far away was the escarpment that fell away over 8,000 feet, down to the Red Sea some 40 miles east. There are thousands of baboons in those cliffs and gorges.

On yet another occasion sometime after that Tsehaitu burst into the house all excited, and she was looking for something with which to catch a "chicken." She led us outside and showed us a beautiful guinea hen. Tsehaitu assured us the bird was delicious to eat and she would cook us up a great chicken dinner. Because I was sure that she would not be able to catch the bird, I didn't stop her from trying. For a week or two the fowl lived in or near our yard and then it too disappeared. Our cliff must have been like a little highway for wildlife. I suppose an animal could make its way along the edge of the cliff for quite a distance, maybe even out of town.

ON THE STRENGTH OF Stanley Bodner's recommendation, we took a one-week vacation the beginning of January, 1974, to the capital city of Yemen, Sana'a. Stanley had gone there several times, and come back loaded down with slides and guns and daggers and silver. We had met a young Peace Corps Volunteer serving in Yemen who had previously come over to Kagnew hospital sick with some sort of bug. She had been accompanied by her Country Director, and they both stayed a few days in Asmara, during which time they invited us to come over and stay with them in Sana'a.

The trip was about an hour by jet, and three hours back by DC3. The DC3 flight was fun; we flew low over the Red Sea and could see coral reefs just below the surface. We had a remarkable visit. We were accompanied on our sightseeing trips by an American Embassy officer in his Land Rover. Sana'a is an old, oddly picturesque city. About as big as Asmara, but it was primitive and dirty by comparison.

Our only other outings that winter and spring of 1974 were a trip to Mekele for a Peace Corps teacher conference, and several trips down to Massawa to visit friends who had a sea-front apartment in the old City. They had a little outboard boat in which we putted out to Green Island to do some snorkeling off the coral reef. I found the ability to see so clearly underwater a little unsettling. Every time a large tuna swam up toward me, I promptly turned around and made for the boat — sharks and barracuda were plentiful around there.

TIME FINALLY RAN OUT FOR ETHIOPIA in February of 1974. The month before, teachers in the schools in Asmara joined with other professionals in the city in a general strike. Cheryl and I did not teach for four weeks. We spent our days visiting Massawa, seeing Asmara, eating lunch at downtown restaurants, visiting the market and shops, and following the progress of the two knotted rugs being loomed for us at the local Orthodox church. But no sooner did we go back to work, than the military coup began. The straw that broke the camel's back was the truck drivers' strike, which followed the cab drivers' strike. Finally, the Ethiopian Army's Second Division enlisted men, headquartered in Asmara, arrested their officers. They then arrested all the provincial government officials and closed the banks and airport. Then the First Division in Addis did the same. Finally, the Navy and Air Force followed suit. All the while, the military was swearing loyalty to His Imperial Majesty, who was being kept under lock and key in the palace.

During this time the Eritrean Liberation Front kidnapped some foreign nurses, killing one in the process. Then they announced open season on all Americans. That was it for the Peace Corps in Ethiopia. Luckily, Cheryl and I had already finished out the school year and we were all packed and ready to leave the country. We arrived in Addis at the end of May, and took the first flight to Nairobi. We travelled for three weeks in Kenya, then finally we bought a cheap charter ticket to London, and began our trek home.

This article was written in 1977 by Mike Banister.

The Game, The Legacy

BY LEO CECCHINI (ASMARA 1962–1964)

WHILE LIVING IN NEW YORK CITY in 1995, a friend urged me to contact the Eritrean Ambassador to the United Nations. I called his office and as soon as I said my name and that I wanted to meet with their ambassador, the woman who answered passed me on to the ambassador himself. I introduced myself by saying, "My name is Leo Cecchini and I served as a Peace Corps . . ." The Ambassador interrupted me by saying, "Leo Cecchini needs no introduction to the Eritrean Liberation Army." I stammered some brilliant answer like, "Well I hope I am well remembered."

I subsequently met with the Ambassador and we became good friends. Our friendship led to my leading an effort by Ethiopian and Eritrean Returned Peace Corps Volunteers to find a peaceful resolution for the lamentable war that broke out between the two countries in 1998 and ended in 2000 with a cease-fire that we helped put in place.

Whenever I think of that call and the ambassador's opening statement I reflect on why I was so well known to him and all the leaders of the Eritrean Liberation Army. It was because my closest relationship with Eritreans came via my being the coach of the soccer team of the school where I had taught as a Peace

Corps Volunteer. Haile Selassie I Secondary School was Asmara's most prestigious school. However, while it was ranked at the top academically, its soccer team was a so-so affair. I had played a bit of soccer as a schoolboy and so I volunteered to coach the team. All were surprised. "What does this American know about our game?" was the most frequent comment.

Well I certainly did not have the excellent skills that my players had, but I did have experience in how to put together a team from having played American football in high school and in college. I put the team on a training schedule with specific times and responsibilities, and worked with a few of the older players, who were the most experienced, to help me choose a team from the dozens of candidates. I also fought for a change in the school league rules that would allow coaches to replace injured players — it was adopted.

To everyone's amazement we won the school league championship that year with an unbeaten record.

Haile Selassie I Secondary School, Asmara, 1963. Coach Leo Cecchini, front row, second from left; Player / Assistant Coach Ogbaselassie, front row, far left.

The players responded well to my instruction and guidance. To everyone's amazement the team won the school league championship that year with an unbeaten record. I became an instant celebrity in the city of some 200,000 as the high school soccer matches were top sporting events. I remember riding my bicycle through some of the more humble sections of the city and having young children run out to greet me screaming, "Cecchini, Cecchini."

THE SECOND YEAR of my Peace Corps service I recall reading a newspaper preview of the coming league soccer season. The writer extolled the virtues of various players and coaches with particular emphasis on the coach of our main rival, Prince Makonnen School, who was a former player for the Ethiopian National Team. But after pumping up all the other schools and their players and coaches the writer simply stated, "But Haile Selassie has Cecchini as its coach." That was it! I was the magician who would field another winning side.

We had a tough season. My team had the infuriating habit of scoring just enough goals to win by a hair. The showdown came when we faced Prince Makonnen. It was a hard-fought game that promised to end in a draw when one of my players kicked a free kick that traced a beautiful arc through the air to pass just between the goal bar and the outstretched hand of the keeper to score the only goal of the game that ended in pandemonium. Fights broke out all over the place and it took all the teachers present some time to quiet down the crowd.

We played a few more games winning by a hair's breadth each time, but ended with another season of no losses, and once again

It was a hard fought game that promised to end in a draw when one of my players kicked a free kick that traced a beautiful arc through the air to pass just between the goal bar and the outstretched hand of the keeper to score the only goal of the game that ended in pandemonium.

winning the League's championship. By now I was national news. Not only had we won two championships, we had also beaten the army and air force teams in Asmara. Haile Selassie Secondary School became the place for promising soccer players to play.

My ambassador friend told me when I first met him that he was still in middle school when I coached at Haile Selassie, but he and all his friends aspired to play for me there. I joked with him that, since I also taught geography, I had probably taught the Liberation Army how to read maps, as well as battlefield tactics on the playing field.

As coach of the school team, I had a very close relationship with the nearly 100 fine young men who tried-out for the team and eventually played. I was also known by all the people in the city. What I left, I found out thirty years later, was a big impression on Eritrea and its people. And it was apparently a good one.

Meeting with My Students

BY NEIL KOTLER (ASMARA 1964–1966)

MY STUDENTS IN ASMARA came to school in ragged clothes eager to learn, and anxious to play a part in their country's development. It was a joy to teach them, and for me to learn from them.

I met with interested students monthly in 1965 and 1966 at my home to discuss school, events in the world, and politics. We also discussed our views on Eritrean independence. These meetings were voluntary and removed from my official duty as a teacher in secondary school.

A lot of our discussions focused on Eritrea where I was stationed as a Peace Corps Volunteer. It had been a United Nations trust territory administered by Great Britain from 1952 to 1962. After the trust dissolved, Eritrea became part of Ethiopia. Eritrea, its fate and its future, were subjects widely talked about in town.

Most of the students favored Eritrean independence. They argued that an independent Eritrea was viable. It had an enormous sea coast that could potentially develop a ship building industry and ports for trade. Eritrea had a modern airport, and the American technology situated at the U.S. base, Kagnew Station, could help propel Eritrea into a modern technological world.

Eritrea had a separatist party but its reach was very limited while I was in the country. There was virtually no active political opposition to the Ethiopian government. The only quasi-political opposition came from the shiftas, bands of terrorists who stole goods from foreigners and others. These terrorists, in the areas where they were active, caused considerable concern. The remarkable winding road from Asmara to Massawa on the Red Sea was one of the most active places where the shiftas operated.

I shall never forget the ambition, grace, and intelligence that characterized my students.

My gatherings with the students were valuable for them. They had a place to express their views and argue with one another freely. They could demonstrate their intellectual acumen and their leadership on issues. They strengthened their own views and developed convictions about them. They could argue with an American teacher who had equally strong views. By the time I left, some students had become members of the separatist party that eventually won independence from Ethiopia.

I have had little communication with the students after I left Asmara, but I shall never forget the ambition, grace, and intelligence that characterized my students. They were impressive human beings. Their presence lifted my Peace Corps experience to a great height.

Physics, Politics and Music

BY CURT PETERSON (ASMARA 1966–1970)

LEARNING THAT I WOULD NOT BE serving in the village of Imdibir, Ethiopia — a "dream location" according to one of the RPCVs working in our Peace Corps training program at Harvard, but would instead be teaching physics in a large secondary school in Asmara, Eritrea, the second largest city in Ethiopia, was initially very disappointing to me. The fact that there were political "shiftas" (bandits) in the Eritrean countryside was portrayed as a drawback to the assignment, but I had actually lamented the urban-living aspect more, as I had been hoping to be the only American teaching in a very small village.

But what flowed from the realities of life in Asmara was a priceless immersion into Eritrean cultures, Ethio-Eritrean politics and the Tigrinya language in a city filled with thousands of friends and acquaintances. My experience became the catalyst for the emergence of my new self-identity. I loved teaching my physics classes, and eventually I even extended my service years out of enthusiasm for a side project that focused my energies on something musical. Though it became somewhat complicated "politically," and was in addition to my physics teaching at Haile Selassie I Secondary School (now Keyih Bahri or Red Sea School), the experiences I had with our "Harambee" group will always live in my cherished memories of my Peace Corps service.

The experiences I had with our "Harambee" group will always live in my cherished memories.

In the spring of 1968, I attended a performance given by a traveling musical group called "Harambee Africa." They were an African continent-wide version of "Up with People," a musical offshoot of the organization MRA (Moral Re-Armament). Several of the "Harambee Africa" musicians (from Uganda, Kenya, Zambia and South Africa) visited our school the next day and invited our students to form our own local "Harambee" musical troupe. My 10th grade physics students, having seen me demonstrate the physics of the vibrating string and knowing that I played a guitar, asked me if I would be their sponsor and help them with the music. We then invited students from the other Asmara secondary schools to join us at our meetings, and soon we had about forty enthusiastic members. Four members expressed interest and aptitude in learning to play guitar, and the rest would be vocal soloists and chorus personnel. Our stage performances also included a "narrator" who gave context to each piece of music and explained things in the languages of the audiences for whom we performed.

In order to expand our rehearsal schedule and to make it easier for members to attend, we shifted our practice space from the stage of our school auditorium to the stage of the Asmara YMCA. Soon we had learned and polished enough songs so that we could perform a full program. We were singing songs in English, Swahili, Tigrinya, and Amharic. Some of the English songs were from the repertoire of "Up with People," and the Swahili pieces were from "Harambee Africa" — the cast of which had members from Kenya and Uganda. Our own members translated, composed and developed lyrics for the songs in Tigrinya and Amharic.

"Harambee Asmara" in performance, Curt Peterson on guitar, front row, second from the left

Word got around — actually, the son of the mayor of Asmara was one of our singers — and soon the Governor General of Eritrea, Ras Asrate Kassa, invited our group to perform at the Eritrean Provincial Palace in central-city Asmara. At the close of that performance the Governor General publicly offered our group a grant of 5000 Ethiopian Birr (at the time the exchange rate was 2½ Birr/US Dollar) to help our troupe to continue to perform both in Asmara and in other parts of the province. We used some of the grant money to buy two electric guitars, an electric bass, amplifiers, microphones, stage risers and colorful African print pullover shirts and hats for the members to wear during performances. We had decided to wear something different from any of the traditional regional costumes in order to both stand out and be more inclusive. The print fabric was obtained from some of the East Indian shops near the Asmara central market, and the colors and patterns were similar to what I had seen on a trip to Nairobi during a summer vacation in 1967.

The grant also made it possible for us to send one of our members to Italy to meet with members of the Italian branch of "Up with People" called "Viva la Gente".

Shortly after the palace performance, I was invited to accompany the Eritrean Minister of Education (the equivalent of a State Superintendent of Schools) to a private audience with Ras Asrate Kassa at the provincial palace. I was looking forward to the meeting with a naïve sort of excitement. The very nervous Minister and I met on the steps of the palace and went in through the outer office reception area. When the door to the Governor General's office was opened, the Minister went down on his knees just inside the door, and I looked to the left to see Ras Asrate Kassa standing tall (he was around 6'4", and standing behind his desk on a broad elevated platform) at the far end of a long carpet with several couches lining each side of his long office. I did not hesitate near the door, but walked straight to the desk and shook his hand. The Minister joined us, and we began discussing the possibility of my staying in Asmara for up to two more years to work with "Harambee Asmara." I asked whether the government would be contracting me to stay. The Ras said he would prefer it if I would remain in Asmara as a Peace Corps Volunteer. At first, I was disappointed to hear this, but I was ultimately very fortunate to have the umbrella of protection that came with the extension of my two-years of my Peace Corps service.

ABOUT A YEAR LATER I was injured in an accident with an Eritrean Police Land-Rover while riding my bicycle, and all my medical care was covered by the Peace Corps. Soon after that I was classified 1-A by my local draft board. The Peace Corps sent me to Italy for a physical exam (as was required for my preparation to be drafted by the U.S. government, even though there was a full medical facility on the military base in the city of Asmara), and also helped me with an appeal of my draft status. Eventually, the draft board assigned my birth date the number 344 out of 366, and they ended up calling-up no one with a number higher than 195. The war in Vietnam required the service of several Peace Corps Volunteers, but I was able to complete my full four years of Volunteer service. The Peace Corps trained me, employed me for four years, took care of my health needs, helped me in the appeal of my 1-A draft classification, and then helped me make a smooth transition "back" to a totally new life in the United States. The "Green Sheet" published by the Peace Corps to connect home-bound Volunteers with work and educational opportunities alerted me to a program in anthropology in upstate New York where I earned an advanced degree and went on to teach in the field at a college for the next thirty-nine years.

"HARAMBEE ASMARA" WAS A GREAT extracurricular organization for me and my students. Each of us loved the opportunities to express ourselves musically, and we gave little thought to the probable political motives behind the Ethiopian governmental blessing and financial support. The troupe elected a slate of officers and they, with minor supervision, conducted our meetings, rehearsals and interactions with the wider community in a very mature and professional manner.

We were able to sing in a variety of venues. In addition to the government-run secondary schools, we performed at a number of locations in Eritrea, including: the Bottego (Italian) secondary school, the Kagnew Station military dependents' school, the Asmara YMCA, the colonial period theater in Mendefera, the open-air colonial theater in Massawa, the Teatro Asmara (a three balcony colonial-construction opera house), and the cafeteria at the Itegue Menen Mental Hospital (now the Eritrean Ministry of Communication). Many of the members had never been to the cities of Massawa or Mendefera, and few had ever been inside most of the Asmara venues where we performed. This was partially due to the fact that travel had become more restricted as the Eritrean liberation struggle became more visible and viable. The government had, in the latter quarter of the 1960s, closed the main roads outside of Asmara to all post-sunset travel, and military personnel accompanied every intercity passenger bus after a few of them had been stopped and burned by the liberation forces.

TWO OF THE TRULY MEMORABLE PERFORMANCES of our group were at Kagnew Station's Robert E. Lee Dependents' School (what a poetic collision of names), and at the mental health hospital campus of the Itegue Menen Hospital (much of the former Itegue Menen Hospital is now called the Orotta Hospital). Each of these performances presented its own unique challenges and opportunities for the growth of all participants (performers, audience and administrators).

We could all see the military base from the back windows of Haile Selassie I Secondary School, but none of our student members had ever been inside its gates. The idea to perform for the "Americans" came from our student officers. So three of us entered the main gate of Kagnew Station on foot and were ushered into the office of the principal of the dependents' school. As the introductions began, the principal, wearing his military uniform, asked me what my "rank" was. I told him I was a teacher with the Peace Corps, and from that point on he addressed me as "Peace Corps," both during our discussion and

The principal, wearing his military uniform, asked me what my "rank" was. I told him I was a teacher with the Peace Corps, and from that point on he addressed me as "Peace Corps."

a week later, at our performance. He never called me "Curt" or "Mr. Peterson" but always used my "rank." In spite of this stiffness with the principal, we set up and had a wonderful performance at the school. There were over 100 students in attendance and our members had never seen that many young Americans in one place. All of us took note of the "little piece of America" feel of the base, right down to the "white picket fences" and freshly mowed lawns of dependent housing. We were all accustomed to seeing the motorcycles and large convertibles driving by our school, but the "Harambee" performance inside the base created a new level of cross-cultural interaction!

The decision to perform at the Itegue Menen Mental Health Hospital ("enda tsululat" or "home of the crazy people" is what the students called it among themselves) was again the suggestion of our group's student leadership. The facility had been a fort built during the Italian Colonial period. The performance took place in the dining room for the patients, and we arrived to set up our instruments and microphones just as the hospital staff began distributing cigarettes for the mid-afternoon "smoke." It seemed as if everyone smoked, and the room soon had a thick cloud of smoke hanging over our somewhat cramped performance area. About twenty-five Harambee members participated, and the whole event was quite an experience for all who were in attendance. The microphone and guitars were a real novelty to the audience and some individuals continually grabbed at the equipment. Our student members confessed after the "concert" that their main struggle was with their own fears of interaction with the hospital patients. Between songs the eyes of the performers showed their levels of concern, but the staff of the facility had a gentle way of keeping things under control without restricting the atmosphere of "spontaneous interaction" flowing out of the patients' responses to our presence. In general, I had found Eritreans to be very comfortable with people that had infirmities and special needs, but the close interaction with this group of about thirty mental patients was a real stretch for all of us!

In KEEPING WITH THE "WORK TOGETHER" theme of the organization, ("Harambee" is a Swahili word meaning "let's work together or pull together") some of our officers suggested that we see if the local orphanage had any needs that a group work-project might be able to address. Following up on the idea, arrangements were made for some of our members to spend a weekend fixing fences, and making or repairing chicken coops and rabbit cages.

At that time in Eritrea's history, the status of "orphan" was a very hopeless status, and their numbers were on a course of dramatic increase as the Ethiopian army was periodically killing families in rural areas that were thought to be supplying food to the liberation movement insurgents. One day while I was visiting Joseph, an Eritrean author/translator/friend in his chronic-ward room at the hospital, (he had been an English teacher and he had become paralyzed as a result of polio, but he continued to be able to translate "Macbeth" and "Hamlet" from Shakespeare's English into very intelligible Tigrinya with good flow) I noticed a young boy with his head wrapped in bandages. Joseph told me the youngster had been left for dead in his home village when Ethiopian forces had come through and shot all the adults, but refused to "waste" the bullets on killing the children. Several such children had been left for dead after being beaten with the soldiers' rifle butts. The so called "collateral damage" caused by war is always beyond comprehension.

Along with such events contributing to the increase in orphan numbers, another sad aspect of orphan status was the fact that once children were separated from their known family members, no other Eritrean would think of adopting them. Without proof of their parentage, these children would spend their lives to the age of legal self-sufficiency as wards of an orphanage.

Harambee Asmara performing community service at the orphanage with some of the children

Our members knew of these things, but those happy afternoons spent with the children and their Catholic nun care-givers were really eye opening. Working on these construction projects in the midst of these orphans made a subtle political statement and intensified our awareness regarding the political realities of the day.

THE ERITREAN STRUGGLE FOR INDEPENDENCE from Ethiopian rule had reached new levels shortly before 1962, when Haile Selassie unilaterally dissolved the Eritrean Parliament and annexed the former Italian colony. Prior to these changes, Eritrea had been through a troubling series of political statuses. During the "Scramble for Africa" of the 1880s, Eritrea was gradually taken and made into a colonial territory by the Italians. In 1896 they attempted to expand their Horn of Africa colonial holdings by invading Ethiopia, and were defeated by Menelik II and his Ethiopian army at the "Battle of Adwa." Years later the defeat at

Adwa inspired Benito Mussolini to lead the Axis Power forces of the Italians in a "revenge motivated invasion" of Ethiopia in 1935. Italian control of "Africa Orientale" ended in 1941 with defeat by the Western Allies and the Ethiopian and Eritrean armies. Eritrea was held as a British Protectorate for the duration of World War II and somewhat beyond. In 1942 the British invited the United States to establish the former Italian Radio Marina as a communications base in Asmara, and this base evolved into Kagnew Station with its considerable war related importance during the Korean and the Vietnam Wars. During the early years of the United Nations, after considerable debate, a decision was made to "gift" the territory of Eritrea to Ethiopia in the form of a federation. Haile Selassie had been a loyal friend to the West, and he had made a claim of Eritrea in a letter presented at the first session of the UN. An Eritrean Assembly and constitution were agreed to by the Emperor of Ethiopia, in 1952, and Eritrea was promised a degree of democratic freedom and autonomy. The U.S. was also given continuing rights to the communications base.

At that time, there were no clearly developed policies regarding the political emergence of African colonial territories. Such policies, formulated during the early 1960s with the independence of several West African colonies, came to recognize the "permanent" legitimacy of colonial boundaries as the official boundaries for the emerging African States. Eritrea's 1941 liberation had been just a partial liberation as a result of this timing issue, and the democratic status of this smaller member of a 1952 federation with Ethiopia eventually deteriorated into a totally unilateral annexation by Ethiopia.

The newly formed U.S. Peace Corps sent an early group of Volunteers to Ethiopia in September of 1962, just three months prior to Ethiopia's forced annexation of Eritrea, and some Volunteers from that first Ethiopian contingent were even sent to Eritrea. This chronology reveals much regarding the arrogant nature of Ethiopia's domination of Eritrea. The Emperor's autocratic control of the political and economic affairs of Eritrea immediately inspired an increasingly militant response from the Eritreans, and he sought ways to, at least, symbolize equity among the regions. The Peace Corps Volunteers he allowed to be sent to Eritrea were his "gift" of Americans to what became the new Ethiopian province. Though my own service years began four years later, many of us "Ethiopia IV" Volunteers still came to Eritrea with very little perspective regarding the nature of and reasons for the Eritrean struggle, let alone the thinly veiled politics of Haile Selassie's constitutional monarchy. I gradually came to understand that Ethiopia's requesting and placing of Volunteers, at least in the Eritrean situation, was very heavily politically motivated.

I also came to see clearly why some Eritrean young people thought that I, and even "Harambee Asmara," were working for the CIA. Such accusations had been common among those struggling, and seeking political separation from colonial rule or imperialism in any of its manifestations. The Peace Corps, Moral Re-Armament, and "Harambee" were all subjected to occasional criticism and scrutiny. In the case of the Eritrean province, in the late 1960s, all three organizations were present in Asmara and other parts of Eritrea at the permission and even the request of the Ethiopian government. Some of the leaders of the Asmara contingent of MRA had, in fact, just come, in early 1968, from the escalating Nigerian factional unrest and burgeoning Biafran Civil War. They had been there at the request of Nigeria's leadership in an attempt to put a lid on the festering of the ethnic, religious and economic inequalities that persisted after decolonization. "Harambee Asmara" never participated in any joint presentations with the MRA representatives, but the Ethiopian Government and its Governor General were, from their points of view, using a variety of "weapons" to try to keep the Eritrean liberation efforts from succeeding.

Kagnew Station's existence in Asmara was another political complication for the Eritrean independence cause. Historically, the base had always remained a communications center (without any serious military might) since its inception as Radio Marina under the Italians, and continued as such after it was officially turned over to the British at the time of the Italian surrender, in 1941. The American presence in Asmara actually began as a secret operation of seven soldiers during World War II, and the flow of American personnel gradually increased until shortly after the 1952 federation of Ethiopia and Eritrea. This union of Eritrea and Ethiopia would make it possible for a Western ally to have dependable access to this highland vantage point for clear communications literally around the world. In 1953 the Base Rights Agreement was signed and the base was renamed after a horse of great spiritual and political significance to Ethiopia.

The word "Kagnew" means "order out of chaos," and the first edition of the "Kagnew Gazelle," the base's own publication, printed the following sentences regarding the history of that legendary horse, "The word Kagnew first appeared in Ethiopian history during the Battle of Adwa in 1896. Kagnew was the name of an Ethiopian general's horse that, riderless, galloped towards the attacking Italians heartening the Ethiopians into repulsing them. Successive attacks by the Ethiopians led by the general mounted on Kagnew defeated the Italians. Ethiopian legend states that St. George rode the horse in the first charge." Though the base's name was noble, the diplomacy connected with keeping access to it required behaviors that were ignoble. Kagnew Station remained an important reason for U.S. indifference regarding the independence struggle of the Eritreans, but also kept our diplomatic alliance with Ethiopia alive. With the 1974 overthrow and eventual death of the Emperor in 1975, Kagnew was living on borrowed time. Mengistu Hailemariam and his Communist military junta, the Derg, eventually abrogated the Base Rights Agreement, and Kagnew Station became but a memory. Financial cuts had already forced the Army personnel to leave by 1973, but the Navy kept the communication link alive until the 1977 unilateral action by President Mengistu. Satellite communications have since removed the need for any such base in this highland region of Africa, but for nearly a quarter of a century Kagnew Station and the Ethiopian Government had danced in a game of political give-and-take in order to keep the strategic base available for crucial U.S. communications purposes. This dance was not always confined to the dance floor, and I was constantly telling people I was a "memhir" or teacher in order to distance myself from the baggage typically associated with this military base.

IN SPITE OF the political dimension of all that was swirling around Asmara during those "golden" four years of my service, 1966 thru 1970, (Eritreans in the diaspora often refer to those years as "gizey worki" or "a golden time" before the escalation of the independence struggle and its aftermath) I was able to easily live with the fact that I was actually teaching very important lessons in physics, and my Eritrean students were going to be better people because they were learning these things. When the opportunity to work with "Harambee Asmara" was added to my teaching activities, the complexities of the politics of being an American in the Peace Corps while serving in Asmara, Eritrea, living near an American military base, became much more intricate. We were singing, at the Ethiopian Governor General's invitation, about "working together" and moving a united Africa forward, but all of us were favoring the liberation of Eritrea at the very same time. Personally, I found it easy to justify my participation given the joys of rehearsing and performing with the membership while encouraging each of them to function as part of a coordinated performance troupe. Music was the draw, and music performance was the goal. A rough draft of Harambee Asmara's constitution, as written by our members, contains the following statement as its second article: "The purpose of this organization shall be to demonstrate the will to hard work, to unite people by changing their motives, to demonstrate that cooperation can be achieved, and Africa, curing division hatred, can develop the world etc." (Yes, that article of the constitution ended with "etc." even in the final draft).

An 11th grade physics class – fall 1968

These ideas were consistent with those promoted by the original visiting "Harambee Africa" company, but our students did not interpret them in the same political way as the Emperor, Governor General or even the Eritrean Minister of Education. The constitution and the lyrics we sang contained messages very much open to a variety of interpretations. Our audiences were free to hear, read and interpret our words in the ways that they wanted. I'm tempted to label the constitutional article and the song lyrics we sang to have been less poetic manifestations of the revered Amharic oral tradition called "wax and gold." Our own message of "working together" was largely about coordination of a group for the purpose of performance or a local work project, and our message of "moving Africa forward" was about valuing education and the economic development of an independent Eritrea. Quite a contrast to the Emperor's desire that we should sing to the youth of Eritrea words which might encourage them to put aside the goal of Eritrean independence from Ethiopia.

There was never any "on stage" agitation for the independence of Eritrea, but the "Harambee Asmara" members were all aware of the design of the flag that would eventually fly over an independent Eritrea. Their political heroes were those living in exile, while inspiring many to revolution with their written and spoken words. Most of our members had relatives fighting with the Eritrean Liberation Front or at least supplying food and other forms of support to the insurgence efforts.

It is logical, but also terribly ironic, that "Harambee Asmara's" unraveling was inadvertently inspired by the paranoid actions of the Ethiopian Government that had welcomed and supported us. A form of martial law was implemented in the winter of 1970, and no gathering of three or more students was allowed outside of the context of school. We were, in effect, forbidden from rehearsing or performing. Even the YMCA and Moral Re-Armament were without participants during the months that followed. The "anti-gatherings" rule was in place to prevent conspiratorial coordination of any disruptive or insurgent activities, but it also prevented any controlled release of the frustrations with HIM Haile Selassie and the Ethiopian Regime.

AS TENSIONS BUILT, students throughout the city of Asmara developed their own coordinated direct-action. The action taken was not led by anyone, nor was it led by any one group. The school-related action started shortly before mid-day in the middle of the week. I had finished teaching my second morning class and had a 45 minute break coming before the next. I decided to cash my monthly Peace Corps paycheck while waiting, so I got on my ten-speed bike and rode it over to the bank. (I had originally "trained" on the mountainous roads north of the city thinking I might try-out for the 1968 Summer Olympics in Mexico City, that plan never came to fruition, but the bike was great transportation.)

Inside the bank there were never any real waiting lines in front of the individual tellers, just a crowd of customers anxious to be served. My approach was usually just to stand at the back, and since I was taller than every other patron, I would eventually be called to the front to cash my check. I would sign my check and the teller would write a number on the back of it and give me a small metal tag with the same number stamped in it. I would then retreat to the back of the crowd waiting for my number to be called in one of four languages (Tigrinya, Amharic, Italian, or English) they commonly used.

I had been waiting to hear my number for about 15 minutes when I decided something was out of the ordinary. I elbowed my way to a teller's desk and asked him in Tigrinya to look for my numbered check. It took him another five minutes, and eventually he was looking in waste-paper baskets. Suddenly, I saw him pluck it from the debris in one of the baskets and then smooth out the wrinkles. He then processed my check and handed me four fifty-birr notes. As bills of larger denominations are virtually worthless in most contexts in the city, I then asked for some smaller change. I was directed to move to a second group huddled near another teller where they were waiting to exchange money. As the time before my class was getting short I stood in the group and inched toward the desk at every opportunity, and was eventually able to receive the change that had I requested.

Smaller bills in my wallet, I rode back to the school and found the entire student body (about 1,200 students) milling around both inside and outside of the main gate to the campus. I asked some of my students about this unscheduled break from classes, and they said they were "on strike."

All of the teachers and school administrators had gathered in the faculty lounge to discuss the events of the morning. Because I was arriving late for my scheduled class time, I arrived last to the faculty lounge out of breath and embarrassed. Everyone seemed to stop mid-sentence as I opened the lounge door and took a seat. I felt as though I had triggered the strike by being tardy for my fourth period physics class even though I knew my lateness was the result of the banking mistake.

The strike lasted for ten weeks and the city of Asmara became a silent "stage" for non-violent student protest. Anti-establishment/anti-war student strikes had recently taken place on college campuses around the U.S., but these were high school students in Africa.

The strike lasted for ten weeks and the city of Asmara became a silent "stage" for non-violent student protest. Anti-establishment/anti-war student strikes had recently taken place on college campuses around the U.S., but these were high school students in Africa. The students did not appear on the campus during the strike, but the faculty gathered every morning and afternoon to be ready for things to get back to normal. We spent many an hour over a chessboard with coffee at the nearby café. The sad part of any strike is the time lost, and these students were shooting themselves in the foot while standing up to their government. This single point of leverage made them pay an even bigger price for the changes that they only hoped might come. After the strike ended, we all worked feverishly to complete the spring term. "Harambee Asmara" had suffered a killing blow, and, at the same time, my four year term of service was swiftly coming to an end.

The Peace Corps remained in Eritrea until 1974 when the Ethiopian head of state Menghistu Hailemariam's struggle with the Eritrean liberation forces began to truly threaten the safety of the Volunteers. Then in 1995 Peace Corps Volunteers began serving in the country of Eritrea shortly after it achieved its independence from Ethiopia. In 1998 the program was again suspended as Isaias Afwerki began pursuing a paranoid course of political isolationism.

I HAVE NOT BEEN BACK TO ASMARA since 1970, but I visit often in my memories and with the thriving Ethiopian and Eritrean communities of the diaspora. I have been able to remain connected with one of the members of "Harambee Asmara." Kassahun Checole, now the owner and publisher of Africa World

Press and The Red Sea Press, was able to come to the U.S. as a student during the period when I was at SUNY Binghamton working on my Masters in Anthropology. He helped me prepare a linguistics paper I submitted on pluralisation in Tigrinya. He went on for his graduate studies at Rutgers University and founded the sister publishing companies some 28 years ago. He says, "Our business mission is to make sure Africans and African Americans have knowledge of "self" as a basis for functioning in today's world." He has published over 1,500 titles on topics focusing on African and African American politics, history and social conditions, and now adds approximately 124 new books each year.

Recently I located, with the help of a network of Eritrean Facebook friends, the first and only president of "Harambee Asmara." Hopefully, this networking will continue and I will be able to make contact with many other former members of our troupe.

I also visit Asmara in a virtual sense through the wonderful systems of Google Maps and Mapygon satellite views of Asmara and its surroundings. All three Asmara houses I lived in are still there, and Youtube continues to surprise me with the sights and sounds of Asmara.

My years in Eritrea redefined my priorities, goals and life's work. I could never repay the Peace Corps or the people of Eritrea, and especially the membership of "Harambee Asmara," for their gifts of support, kindness, wisdom and patience. Thank you!

I could never repay the Peace Corps or the people of Eritrea, and especially the membership of "Harambee Asmara," for their gifts of support, kindness, wisdom and patience. Thank you!

Never Repeated . . . Never Forgotten

BY LOIS SHOEMAKER (ASMARA 1962–1964)

IMAGINE MY DELIGHT when my Denver, Colorado, book club chose *Cutting For Stone* by Abraham Verghese as one of our selections to read this year. It is a terrific fictional story, and as I read it, I recognized so many things. Perhaps most striking for me was the sentence " . . . the probationer had from a young age addressed her self-consciousness by becoming excessively studious, a trait encouraged

Time spent at Itegue Menen Hospital Orphanage in Asmara

by the Italian nuns, the Sisters of the Nigrizia (Africa), who raised her in the [Itegue Menen Hospital] orphanage in Asmara." As Peace Corps Volunteers assigned to Asmara, my husband, Terry (1937–1975), and I lived in an upstairs apartment in an Italian-built building located near the orphanage. The orphanage was one of my favorite places to go — to be with the young children living there.

SO MANY DAY-TO-DAY OPPORTUNITIES, and just plain "living/sharing life" began to take place for us in Asmara in September 1962. Terry and I were both assigned to Haile Selassie I Secondary School — Terry to teach math, and I, home economics. Teaching math in Eritrea was similar to teaching it in the U.S., but teaching home economics — a whole new concept in the classroom there — was a challenge. I avoided teaching "Foods" as I had in the U.S., but found a way to work on nutrition, health and personal growth for the girls at the secondary school. I also enjoyed helping some of the girls at a near-by elementary school with their English. Perhaps most important, though, was the time I spent with each child, sharing our lives.

TERRY AND I WERE BOTH INVOLVED with extra activities, including Scouting programs loosely modeled after the U.S. Boy Scout/Girl Scout programs.

Terry had a very successful woodworking club at school that met during the lunch hour. Somehow he had all the necessary tools donated, and then began teaching the boys how to use them. They made U.S.-style ironing boards out of Peace Corps shipping crates, and then sold them to the Peace Corps Volunteers. The goal: to earn money to be able to buy more wood so that the students could build a table, a chair, or a cupboard for their own home. Fellow Volunteer Ray Capozzi was a part of this successful club.

Taboto wearing her pink dress

The two preschool-aged children of our grounds-keepers became my special little friends. I made a pink dress for Taboto that she wore every day.

Shortly before we were to leave Asmara and return home, Taboto's mother appeared at our door. With tearful eyes and hands clasped together in what seemed like a prayer to me, she asked as best she could "would you please take Taboto home with you to America?" As long as I live, I will not forget that mother's pleading look and unspeakable love to want to make a better life for her young daughter.

MARVELOUS, CLOSE friendships were made in Asmara and continue to this day — including with one particular student and his family, all seven of whom are now successful, U.S. citizens. I recently learned that they had "figured out what that bottle of pills was that was kept on our kitchen table" — my birth-control pills! It was also reported that our student's mother asked him, "do you think you can get a pill for me?" — she had already given birth to seven children. No wonder she asked!

I will never forget our last evening in Asmara and our dinner together at this family's home. All of us gathered around the messeb as we enjoyed the zigini dinner together. As we finished, the family huddled together and sang a tearful "God Be With You 'Til We Meet Again." It is now 49 years later, and I can recall that scene as clearly as it if was yesterday. Memories of Asmara, never repeated . . . never forgotten.

Remembrances of Asmara

BY JUDY SMITH (1963–1965)

I REMEMBER ARRIVING in Asmara as a Peace Corps Volunteer teacher in 1963 on a bus. Riding through its lovely tree-lined streets with traffic lights, big American cars along with horse-drawn garis, telephone wires and electricity — I broke down in tears. Of course my husband, Dane, and the other PCVs thought I was crazy, but this was not my Peace Corps dream. I wanted to be out in a hut, roughing it. Instead, as one of the few married couples in our group of new Volunteers, we were put into the recently-vacated house of a former Peace Corps staff member up a hill in Addis Alem.

Well, I got used to it, but, I have to admit, that first year I did not feel like a Peace Corps Volunteer — age 22, just out of college, with a 3 bedroom/2 bath house and a garden. I remember rattling around in that big, concrete block house and asking Dane to come into the bathroom to read while I took a bath. It was lonely.

But we liked our jobs, both of us teaching night classes at the Haile Selassie I University Extension held at the Haile Selassie Secondary School, which was a short way beyond the road that led to Kagnew Station. I taught English to students who were all older than myself, and there were only one or two women.

Dane taught history and political science, the latter being very popular with all of the budding young revolutionaries. We both taught middle school during the day — I at Godaif, where my 6th-grade English students sat three in a desk and couldn't figure out why I objected to their sharing their knowledge during tests, and Dane eventually at the Islamic Benevolent Middle School, which was the beginning of his interest in Islam.

MY MEMORIES OF ASMARA center mostly around food. I remember going to the cheese shop for provolone, the coffee shop and the butcher shop, having learned enough Italian to get along there, and enough Tigrinya to go to the market for fruits and vegetables. Dane, on the other hand, studied both Italian and Arabic, learning enough to build into working languages he has used in his Foreign Service career.

And the Italian restaurants! Another reason we could not think of ourselves as suffering in the Peace Corps. We couldn't believe our good fortune to be able to eat a four-course Italian meal for just 4 or 5 birr. Our favorite was San Georgio for lasagna, veal piccata and crema caramella. We also loved the cafes where we could stop for a café latte or gelati any time of day or evening.

FOR OUR SECOND YEAR we requested a move to a village. Just when we heard that the transfer was granted, we learned that we were pregnant — one of those unplanned and "forbidden" Peace Corps babies. The Peace Corps policy then was that a pregnant woman could stay if she was in a healthy enough place, and could continue her Peace Corps work. Our pregnancy was the third in our group of seven married couples, and our baby, the second to be born at Kagnew Station. I remember riding

Judy and Dane with Jennifer and their university students

my bicycle up to the hospital (before the doctor took away my wheels at 7 months) for pre-natal visits. We were only allowed to use Kagnew Station for medical treatment and church on Sunday, but I remember one illegal — but delicious — chocolate milkshake there. Of course our Eritrean friends were delighted with the idea of our having a baby, but several expressed a fear that "the condition of the air would turn him black." Well, they were mistaken because Jennifer arrived, rosy and healthy, and admired by all, especially our Eritrean friends. Dane and I continued our teaching, staggering our schedules so that one of us could stay with her.

We left Asmara when Jennifer was five months old, and traveled home through Asia for a month — a good start for the first of two of our three children who later became Peace Corps Volunteers themselves. Jenny was a PCV in Cameroon and has returned to Africa in her career with Catholic Relief Services.

M AGICAL MOMENTS in Asmara include —

- Celebrating our first married Christmas, shopping with all the Italian lights and decorations, bringing home our first Christmas tree on our bicycles, Dane holding the small bottle-brush tree out in front like a sword;

- Me whizzing down the Addis Alem hill on my bike going off to teach in the late afternoon;

- The teachers' picnic at Godaif where I received the sheep's eyeball as honored guest and managed to swallow it down;

- Hearing of John F. Kennedy's assassination on the radio at a Peace Corps party, with everyone leaving in shock to go home to cry in private; and then going to the American Embassy to sign the condolence book with crowds of Eritreans showing their respect and affection.

OUR TWO YEARS as Peace Corps Volunteers in Eritrea were the beginning of thirty years in the Foreign Service. During seventeen of those years we lived in seven African countries; during six of those years Dane served as a United States ambassador to two different countries. It was in Asmara, at the U.S. Embassy, that Dane took the Foreign Service exam, after we decided that maybe God would be just as happy with him as a Foreign Service Officer as he would with him as a Methodist preacher. It has been a good choice, and it all began in Eritrea.

Decamere

A Christmas Letter

BY CATHIE HULDER (DECAMERE 1964–1966)

Dear Family and Friends,

I should begin by saying that one of the biggest jobs of a Peace Corps Volunteer is writing letters home. Forgive me for not having written sooner! Although this is meant to convey Christmas greetings, you will probably not receive this letter until after Christmas.

After eleven months in Ethiopia, I am still happy that I decided to come, and I continue to find my new home here quite interesting and comfortable. A year ago I wasn't too sure how I would feel after eleven months, since people say that toward the end of the first year, things begin to drag. Fortunately it hasn't happened to me so far.

I hope this won't disappoint those of you who have pictured the noble Cathie building roads and digging latrines in primitive African villages, but my job so far has been as an English and science teacher in a Junior Secondary School. The Peace Corps' work in Ethiopia is chiefly teaching in the Empire's public schools. This work is being carried out by about 500 Volunteers at present. As most of you know, our term of service lasts approximately two years, so this gives us plenty of time to learn about the country.

Ethiopia is a monarchy ruled by His Imperial Majesty Haile Selassie I, who claims his right to the throne as a descendant of King Solomon and the Queen of Sheba. The country has its own language, Amharic, the oldest written African language outside of Egypt — going back more than 1000 years; its own Christian religion, the Ethiopian Coptic Church, the first religion to be developed by an African people (also well over 1000 years ago); its own calendar system, used everywhere in the Empire, which has 13 months to the year that begins during our month of September (it is now the third month of the year 1958 — E.C.); its own system of time (not practiced in larger cities), where 1:00 comes 1 hour after sunrise, and 12:00 at sunset; and its own national food, called wat. The food is called zigini here in Eritrea, and is a very peppery-hot, chili-like dish eaten with the fingers (right hand only) by dipping up the mixture in a grey, spongy, pancake-like sour bread. In spite of that unappetizing description it really tastes very good!

The economy of Ethiopia rests chiefly on farming and cattle-raising, and most of the people are herdsmen. The country itself is beautiful — rugged and mountainous, looking from the air like one continuous Grand Canyon. And the weather is perfect — sunny and cool all 13 months of the year.

I live in Eritrea, the northernmost province, whose people for the most part don't like to consider themselves a part of Ethiopia, and every now and then there are little grumbles of revolution. In this part of the country are the "shiftas" — highwaymen who rob cars, trucks, buses and sometimes shoot people. They are the reason the U.S. Consulate has told us to stay off the roads between 5:00 p.m. and 7:30 a.m. each day. A few weeks ago our town bus was held up, which caused quite a little excitement around here.

And that now brings me to the town I live in, Decamere, a very pleasant community, which was originally built by the Italians and later deserted by them during World War II. Because so many buildings have been left standing but not inhabited since the Italians left, the place has the appearance of a ghost town. However, recently the town has been undergoing a "re-paint Decamere" campaign and it's beginning to take on the look of some sort of Mediterranean health spa. Some parts of the town, especially the market area with its mosque and frequent camel trade, have a very Arabian flavor, as does all of the rocky and sandy area surrounding Decamere.

There are seven Peace Corps Volunteers in town, and one of the other women and I share a 5-room apartment above (of all things) a grocery store. We both teach 8th grade subjects in the government school on a 33-hour/week schedule. When we aren't preparing lessons, we usually find plenty to do in our off-hours, like getting together with other teachers and friends, or going to the Decamere Cinema for a rousing Italian Spectacular.

Other things contribute to our more interesting moments in Decamere. For instance, every now and then comes a religious Feast Day or wedding celebration with drums and dancing through the streets. On a more solemn occasion, a "walking obituary," as we call him, will come through town and on each street corner call out three times in an eerie wail that someone has died.

Asmara, the capitol of Eritrea and a beautiful city, is only an hour away by bus, and we often go there to buy food and other things we need. The ride in the bused, which look like they were made in 1920, is an experience in itself, what with goats and furniture and bicycles loaded on top, and chickens and water jugs and people inside. We manage to survive each trip in pretty good shape though.

During our two-year stay in the country, all PCV's are required to work on some sort of special project for a month during the school summer break. Last summer I went to Asmara for my project to study the Eritrean language, Tigrinya, and on the side I helped out once in a while at a school that some other PCVs were repairing. It was fun, and it was no time at all until August arrived, our month of vacation.

Five of us took the three-day bus trip to Addis Ababa, the capitol city of Ethiopia, and there we boarded a flight to Nairobi, Kenya. We spent a few days there, then rented a car and indulged in our own 5-day safari through the game parks of Kenya and Tanzania. Two friends and I spent 5 days after that climbing to the top of Mt. Kilimanjaro and down again, which I'm sure is the most tremendous experience I've ever had. After our blistered feet had recovered, the five of us met again in Nairobi and traveled south to Zambia and Rhodesia where we spent a couple days at Victoria Falls. Our travels then took us further on down to South Africa, another very interesting episode of our trip. Seeing apartheid at first hand was quite different, I found, than reading about it in newspapers — shocking in fact, in a country so much like our own, and enforced by people whom we found otherwise to be very hospitable and friendly. Our trip ended a month after it had started, and we probably would have been completely exhausted had it not been for the eight days we spent on the beach in Durban, South Africa, before returning to Ethiopia.

So with that, I conclude this report on the first year I've spent here in Africa. I hope that some of you will send me reports of your own, since I do enjoy hearing about what's going on in the U.S., and especially in the lives of you, my friends and family.

Love, Cathie

Keren

Moments That Change Your Life Forever

BY JOANNE FELDMAN RICHARDS (KEREN 1966–1968)

I JOINED THE PEACE CORPS in 1966 at the ripe old age of 21, just after graduating from the University of Wisconsin at Madison. My group's three-month training program, which took place in Cambridge, Massachusetts, introduced us to the language and customs of our host country, Ethiopia, and reacquainted us with the history and political science of the U.S. As we prepared for life in a very foreign land, we became a close-knit group. I was posted to Keren in Eritrea (the northernmost of all the towns where Volunteers served), but my friends were distributed all over Ethiopia. Before we departed from Addis Ababa to our far-flung cities, towns, and villages, many of us exchanged addresses. In those days there were no cell phones and no email! How would we survive?

Some months into my adventure, I received a letter from Ham Richards, another Cambridge trainee, who was teaching high school physics in Dire Dawa. He really didn't see much future in that — the textbook dated from the 19th Century, and most of the students cared only about passing the School Leaving Exam — but he pressed on. We exchanged more letters, and our courtship was facilitated by our two required Peace Corps meetings, one in the winter of 1966 in Asmara and the other in the summer of 1967 in Addis Ababa.

Fall 1967 brought Ham a lot closer, when he moved to Mekele to work on an irrigation project with the local farmers. Continuing to exchange letters, we also spoke by telephone each Friday. What an experience that was! In those days, long-distance calls were set up piecemeal by human operators, and the operators in Mekele and Keren got so used to our calls that they started to place them without being asked (they were probably eager for the entertainment!). The telephone in Keren was in the post office, to which I was summoned by a runner when the call came through. Every third weekend Ham would travel north from Mekele and I would travel south from Keren to meet in Asmara, ostensibly for appointments with the dentist. By December, having gotten to know each other pretty well, we decided to spend our winter break together exploring the wild animal parks of Kenya and Tanzania. Before leaving for the East African wilderness, we spent a few days in Malindi on the Indian Ocean, and there, on January 6, 1968, Ham asked me to marry him. What a glorious way to begin a wonderful vacation!

PREPARATIONS FOR OUR JULY 4TH WEDDING in Keren were a bit of a challenge. By then the Eritrean Liberation Front was in full force, and the Ethiopian Army was doing its best to crush it. To deny supplies to the ELF, the Army was keeping track of foodstuffs sold in the marketplace; how would we provide refreshments to our guests? Word got around town pretty quickly — students do get excited — that there would soon be a ferenj wedding. Each day the shopkeepers would put

To ——————————————
Miss JOANNE and Mr. HAM
are inviting you to celebrate with them their Marriage on July 4, 1968 from 3:00 to 6:00 in our house by the market.

Thank you.
Miss Joanne and Mr. Ham

away a little bit of sugar, coffee, and sweets, not enough for the Ethiopian Army to notice, but just enough to accumulate over the weeks. A tailor designed my dress by showing me a Sears catalog and having me point to the neckline I wanted — the sleeves, the bodice, the skirt. We picked a fabric. Then he took a scissors and a piece of butcher paper and proceeded to cut out a pattern. It was perfect. The students had wedding invitations printed. I typed seven original marriage certificates.

The bride and groom

July 4th arrived!

The wedding almost went without a hitch. The mayor was to conduct the ceremony, but it was his first ever, and he was so nervous that he forgot all of his English. Fortunately the high-school headmaster was there and stepped in!

Although the formalities took only a few minutes, the celebration afterwards spanned the better part of two days. First came the town officials to pay their respects, then the teachers, and finally the students.

To be on the safe side, the mayor stationed a few police officers to guard the house while the festivities were going on. As the afternoon passed into the evening, the students were dancing to the beat of drums, and then there came a knock and commotion at my compound gate. A drunken Ethiopian Army officer, suspicious that the drums were signaling the ELF, tried to enter while brandishing a gun, but was stopped by the guards. The guards were so concerned, they wouldn't let any of the students go out on the streets — so we partied all night!

One of the drummers and some of the wedding guests

The next morning when Lijajet, my cook, came to prepare breakfast, she was taken aback to see not the half dozen people she was expecting, but more like fifty! With her usual good humor, she found enough food to prepare breakfast for all of us. When the festivities were over, we were all exhausted, but extremely relieved and happy!

FAST-FORWARD 43 YEARS

Ham and I remain happily married, and we still hear from some of those who celebrated with us back on July 4, 1968. Email has kept friendships alive. Some are in the U.S., others in England, Sudan, and Eritrea.

But the story doesn't end here. In August 2011, I received a call from Yohannes Drar, a Keren expatriate who now lives in Ontario, Canada. It turns out that every few years he organizes a Keren High School Reunion in Washington D.C. I plan to attend the next reunion in July 2012, and be reunited with teachers and students many of whom I haven't seen since 1966! What a kick that will be!

These are moments that changed my life forever — in a wonderful way!

Kudo-Abuor

Images and Memories

by Kate Yocum (Kudo-Abuor 1997–1998)

In A BOX IN MY HOME in Portland, Oregon, I keep my Eritrea things. These are some of my things that were nearly left behind during the chaos and confusion of the spring of 1998, when the BBC Africa service — my link to the outside world — reported skirmishes on the border between Eritrea and Ethiopia. Over the next few weeks the skirmishes threatened the peace and security of the country and led to the eventual evacuation of Peace Corps Volunteers and other foreign nationals. By summer, the seven years of peace after a three-decades-long war of independence ended.

My box of belongings arrived in the U.S. a few months after I did. In it, I have my recipe book, a collection of everything that can be made from honey, tomatoes, onions, flour (with or without little black bugs), sugar, and zeiti – vegetable oil. I have my Tigrinya language training book. I have a copy of The Shugurti, an Onion-style "news" letter that I wrote with fellow Volunteers. I have a clay shiro pot that miraculously avoided being broken. My djebena only vaguely recalls the boiling of coffee inside her belly.

We were part of the third batch of Peace Corps Volunteers who were sent to Eritrea after the war that brought independence from Ethiopia. Even though the Peace Corps hadn't been able to place Volunteers in Eritrea during war time, we were able to pick up where the early Volunteers from the 1960s and '70s had left off, and many Eritreans remember being taught by American teachers who served there during Peace Corps' early days while Eritrea was an annexed province of Ethiopia after the Second World War.

In Mendefera, the city where we had our initial nine-week training, our neighbors wore t-shirts commemorating their countrymen and women who lost their lives for Eritrea's liberation. The music in the bars and cafes told their stories. Our hosts made us coffee and injera and helped us with our burgeoning Tigrinya. A half dozen years since the brutality of war and here we were among the most peace-loving people. These were magical months as trainees at San Giorgio Secondary School. Forty-one teachers were in training learning survival Tigrinya and methods for teaching multi-age classes of seventy-five students. In the late afternoon we would walk to town and have a beer at the Merkeb and process all that we heard, tasted, smelled, and learned that day.

What is your name?

My girlfriends and I soon adopted the habit of walking arm and arm in town, just like the Eritrean women — and men. We got used to children shouting "Italian!" and "What is your name?" (Saying my name never seemed to be an adequate response to that question as it was immediately asked of me again by my inquirer.) When we learned enough Tigrinya, we were able to provide more complete answers, "Ane kab America metsie" — I'm American, not Italian — but that didn't have much of an effect. My fellow Volunteer, Eric, decided to supply more imaginative responses such as "Ato Mastika shmey. Kab werhi metsie." ("My name is Mr. Chewing Gum. I come from the moon.") A chance to apply our language training, and hear squeals from the kids.

Weary women, camels, donkeys, and roosters slung atop buses headed south from Mendefera down the Adi Quala road after each market day. Eventually, I joined them, with a bed frame and mattress slung atop the bus that drove south for sixteen kilometers, and then turned west, spending a couple of hours traversing the next sixteen kilometers to Kudo-Abuor, "the place where the oxen rest."

Kate with two of her students

There was not much rest for the oxen, the villagers, or the school teachers over the next eight months in Kudo-Abuor. This was hardscrabble village life, with too many fields to plow and too many children to teach. Too many children visiting my house, too many scorpions to avoid, too much coffee to drink, too many exercise books to correct. Too much rain in the rainy season, too much chica sticking to the bottoms of my sandals. Too many rocks to clear, too many kilometers to the well, too many flies buzzing about, too many little black bugs in my flour. So many students' names to learn; so many hot, dry days; so many gorgeous sunsets. It was all too much, in the warmest and most peaceful way.

EACH NIGHT I WENT TO SLEEP at nine o'clock due to a lack of light, then woke up early, gathered my students' exercise books and headed to school. I would see 325 students during the day, seventh-graders who ranged from twelve to twenty-two years old. God only knows what they made of me, but we found common ground in our desire to be there, working together, learning the English curriculum, and having a few laughs. Looking back, teaching was part chaos, part magic, but it was the beginning of my career in education and I haven't looked back since. They always say that the Volunteer learns more than the hosts, and this was certainly true for me.

I SENT HAND-WRITTEN LETTERS to my Volunteer friends in Senafe, Adi-Kayih, and Tsa'ada Cristian. They were addressed "Amanda, Senafe," stuffed in an envelope, and handed off to the bus leaving the village that day. They contained instructions for a rendezvous two week's hence: "American Bar, noon." And then, two weeks later, there she'd be, drinking a cappuccino on Liberation Avenue. We'd embrace and I'd marvel at the fact that our low-tech communication methods worked, and that I made it to Asmara by noon after leaving Kudo-Abuor on the 4:30 am bus. Other American volunteers would be there too, or they'd just walk by and join us. Our Asmarino friends would find us and later on we'd go dancing at Sembel Huts or search for the one biet megbi where we found falafel once. I loved walking the streets of Asmara, under the palm trees, on the patterned sidewalk tiles. Asmara was the experimental canvas for the art deco architects of Italy, their experiments a bit worse for wear.

The old Italian colonial ghosts found a home in these places, like the Cinema Impero and the old Fiat building. Those ghosts are baked each morning in the Italian bread, and spoken with all of the words for things invented after the end of the nineteenth century.

GOING EAST FROM ASMARA, you drop out of the highlands, wind through the only stretch of forest that I ever saw in Eritrea, through the oasis of Ghinda, hairpin turns the whole way. Finally the landscape flattens and you realize again that it's much, much hotter than you think you can tolerate. That's when you know you are approaching Massawa. People take their cots outside in the streets to try and get some rest, and I walked the streets like a zombie, dizzy from the heat. The colors light blue and white fill my mental canvas when I think of Massawa, a town of flaking plaster without right angles.

SCORPION STING

Some scorpions are far more poisonous than others. To adults, scorpion stings are rarely dangerous. Take aspirin and if possible put ice on the sting to help calm the pain. For the numbness and pain that sometimes last weeks or months, hot compresses may be helpful (see p. 193).

To children under 5 years old, scorpion stings can be dangerous, especially if the sting is on the head or body. In some countries scorpion antitoxin is available (p. 388). To do much good it must be injected within 2 hours after the child has been stung. Give acetaminophen or aspirin for the pain. If the child stops breathing, use mouth-to-mouth breathing (see p. 80). If the child who was stung is very young or has been stung on the main part of the body, or if you know the scorpion was of a deadly type—seek medical help fast.

Where There Is No Doctor — *p. 106*

DURING THESE ELEVEN MONTHS I read and reread my copy of *Where There Is No Doctor*, trying to determine whether it was the small or big scorpions that administered a more painful sting. We Volunteers joked about breaking a tooth so we could have an all-expenses-paid vacation to a "real city" like Nairobi.

In the end we left Eritrea unwillingly and far earlier than we were ready. Leaving as suddenly as we did was one of my most difficult life experiences. I had spent almost a year with my students and had finally learned their names. I wanted to spend another summer in country working on a new project and have

**I left behind people
I loved and in some
cases, didn't get to say
goodbye.**

the opportunity to improve my teaching with the next year's class. I left behind people I loved and in some cases, didn't get to say goodbye.

ERITREA IS NOT A PLACE that is easy to get back to. But I managed — after I finished my master's degree in international education. I had spent the intervening two-and-a-half years studying the country that so fascinated me, and worked to get my career in education that my little village school had inspired off the ground.

Asmara in January was colder than I remembered it. Massawa was just as hot. And Kudo-Abuor, the place where I was not just "Italian!" but "memher" — teacher — was as lush and welcoming as it had been when I arrived with my bed frame on the roof of the bus. Most of the teachers were still there even though they had taken a pay freeze (that is, not arriving at all). Some of my former students were studying at San Giorgio Secondary School where I had done my studies during training. Others would soon be off to Sawa — military training. Many of my colleagues would find a way to the U.S. or South Africa, though some would stay and carry on in an increasingly repressive society. Though the landscape was the same, the people's faces betrayed their disappointment that their country was so soon back at war.

I WAS ONE OF THE LUCKY ONES to live in Eritrea during peace time. In the long memories of people who have been pushed to the edge again and again, I fear that this short but special time will be eclipsed by years of struggle. It feels so easy for me to conjure the images and memories that are so rich and comforting, as my Eritrea is frozen in time as a place liberated from war and not looking back. May those hopeful times sustain the spirits of all Eritreans at home and abroad, as well as us Volunteers who were fortunate enough to be sent there in the late '90s for an experience we will treasure for the rest of our lives.

Mendefera

Generosity

BY HAROLD FREEMAN (MENDEFERA 1965–1967)

Yemane

BACK IN THE 1960s, when what is now the nation of Eritrea was still part of Ethiopia, a student from a village far out in the Eritrean countryside lived with three Peace Corps Volunteers miles away from his home in a town that might be considered the county seat. It was called Mendefera. He lived there so that he could attend the town secondary school, which was the only one in the region. The student, whose name was Yemane, was fortunate to be able to go to the school because at that time only a very small fraction of Ethiopians could read and write.

Eventually Yemane invited the Volunteers, all of whom taught at his school, to visit his village so they could see his home, and so his mother and little brothers could meet the people with whom he lived.

The student and his three teachers rode their bikes for ten or twelve miles along a narrow, but paved, highway. They then turned off onto a dirt road that gave way to what was basically a bumpy path with lots of rocks alongside. Two or three miles of that took them to the village and to Yemane's family's one-room house.

The home had a dirt floor, and for seating there was a hard-packed earthen bench around the wall. In the middle of the floor was a small stove. Yemane's mother had to squat in front of it to do the cooking. She had prepared a fine meal — one rare for ordinary folks because it included stewed chicken and boiled eggs. Such a feast was usually reserved for holidays.

Yemane's mother prepares tea — photo by Mary Gratiot Schultz

The visitors were introduced to other residents of the village, were treated like honored guests, and were well fed. Then, when it came time for them to leave, Yemane's mother presented them with eggs, a parting gift. The Peace Corps Volunteers hesitated, knowing that she and her younger sons needed the eggs much more than they did. However, they were also aware of the Ethiopian and Eritrean traditions of hospitality and generosity, and they could not offend their hostess by simply declining this gift. Thinking that they were being both truthful and clever, they explained that because the road was so bumpy, the bouncing bicycles would break the eggs and they would be wasted.

Yemane's mother accepted this line of reasoning, and the Peace Corps Volunteers felt relief. Until she said, "Then you must take the chicken."

Things Matter in Ways We Never Imagine

BY CYNTHIA TSE KIMBERLIN (MENDEFERA, ASMARA 1962–1964)

WHEN I FIRST THOUGHT ABOUT JOINING the Peace Corps, I never thought being an American of Chinese descent would matter at all. But it did, and not in ways I could have imagined.

Up until then I had never traveled outside the United States, rarely outside California, but I longed to travel to far off places. I spent my formative years growing up in San Francisco with my parents and older sister and younger brother. Although my mother graduated from Northwestern University as a dual English and philosophy major, and worked in a Chinese souvenir shop in Chicago's Chinatown, my father did not allow her to work for monetary compensation after they married. Like many women of her generation born in China, she was not given the opportunity to be on her own from the time she was born to the time she married. My father was also born in China, and came to the United States as a teenager from a village near Canton in Quandong Province not knowing one word of English. He became a physician, and served for nine years on a Navaho Indian Reservation in Ganado, Arizona where I was born. He joined the U.S. Army as a medical field physician, was eventually promoted to Lieutenant Colonel while in the Reserves, and later worked for the Veterans' Administration in

San Francisco. While I was a college undergraduate my father offered me this sage advice: "No matter what you become or how smart or well educated you are, people will look at your face and still think of you first as a Chinese."

My desire to see a world that I had yet to experience was answered when a friend confronted me with the simple but direct admonishment — since I was interested in seeing the world, would I have the nerve to do something like join the Peace Corps? I met his challenge by applying at the end of my junior year in college and the following year, as I was about to graduate, I received a telegram stating that I had been accepted into a Peace Corps training program at a university back east, and that I would be a teacher and a member of the first group going to Ethiopia. I was thrilled.

While I was growing up I was led to believe that I was not even a real American. It wasn't anything people said in particular, but it was made clear by their attitudes, and on occasion people referred to me as "that Chinese girl." I remember junior high school civics class during a lesson about citizenship. The teacher assigned each student to a category, and without asking me, assigned me to the "Chinese," not the "American," category. So it was that as I prepared to depart for training, and I received my first passport, I saw, stated in print on an official document, that I was an American with all the privileges of citizenship. That was a revelation.

I SHARE HERE INCIDENTS that I encountered as a Volunteer and later in my professional career that illustrate realities as I perceived them — by what I experienced, how I felt, and what I was thinking at the time. To my knowledge, I was the first Asian American woman to serve in the United States Peace Corps, and my reminiscences evoke what it was like to be a second generation American who heeded the late President John F. Kennedy's call to service, and to have the privilege to see and hear him speak to my training group on a windy afternoon in the Rose Garden on the White House lawn before leaving for my two-year tour of duty.

EYE-E-E-E-E DON'T GO! (1962)

Except for my paternal uncle, my entire family was aghast and horrified at what I was planning to undertake, and they opposed this endeavor from the start. When I announced I was conditionally accepted into the Peace Corps and was going to train at Georgetown University in Washington, D.C., their response was . . . dead silence. After my parents let this information sink in, they said, "think of this trip to Georgetown as a nice free vacation."

Except for my paternal uncle, my entire family was aghast and horrified at what I was planning to undertake, and they opposed this endeavor from the start.

After training, I returned home and told my family I was leaving for Africa in a few days. Again, they tried to persuade me not to go. My father even called my uncle at three in the morning pleading with him to talk to me saying "you are the only one she will listen to." The stereotypes from well meaning family members and friends came tumbling out — "you'll never get married," my mother wept. Another said, "There are jungles and animals out there," and a myriad of other remarks I would like to forget. But my uncle said to me, "If I were your age, I would go with you." And so I went. (Suffice it to say, one year later after my family watched me on television in the first of a two-part television documentary narrated by Walter Cronkite entitled "The Lion of Judah,"[1] they revised their opinions about Ethiopia and about my decision to join the Peace Corps.)

Shortly after arriving in Ethiopia I commenced my two-year tour of service as a teacher of science and history at St. George Middle School in Mendefera. After school I taught music as my academic training was in ethnomusicology. In addition, I also taught English to working adults.

Cynthia (second from the left) and fellow Peace Corps Volunteer Jacqueline Woodson Ferrill (to right of Cynthia) chaperoning on a field trip with some of their students who were scouts from St. George Middle School, Mendefera, 1963

PEBBLES AND STONES... (1963)

After teaching in Mendefera for a year, I was transferred to a town called Decamere where I was to spend my second year along with another Volunteer teaching English at the local secondary school. Before school commenced, I realized I needed to purchase some household items. On market day, when sell-

Many years later I was
informed that people
said my features —
especially my eyes —
looked strange, and
therefore I must be some
kind of a witch.

ers and buyers came from all over the region, I decided to buy some kitchenwares. After purchasing a few items and walking about, I began to be pelted with pebbles and stones. In startled confusion I soon realized I was being stoned. When my Peace Corps colleague heard about this incident, she became more alarmed than I, and immediately reported it to the Peace Corps Director. Since the Peace Corps did not want this episode to escalate into an international incident, I was transferred out of the area two days later to the more cosmopolitan city of Asmara. Apparently, the people of Decamere had never seen an Asian woman before — and one who was going around telling folks she was an American teacher to boot.

Many years later I was informed that the people in Decamere said my features — especially my eyes — looked strange, and therefore I must be some kind of a witch. At the time, I felt sorry for those who had done this to me, and that they had done it out of ignorance about foreigners, because of their customs and because of their lack of knowledge about the diverse people living in America.

Since then, I have recommended to the American Embassy and the expatriate community that they make greater efforts to educate Ethiopians about the diversity of people in America — and around the world. As recently as 1996, a young Chinese American Fulbright Scholar who lived in a town south of Addis Ababa, told me that she had felt "harassed every minute of every day" that she was there because she looked different from other Americans. Unfortunately, Ethiopians and Eritreans still tend to perceive most Americans through the narrow lens of a black/white dichotomy.

Separate but not equal (1963)

In 1963 I was not aware of South African apartheid and its devastating effect on the entire country. But it was about to affect me profoundly.

A number of Peace Corps Volunteers with whom I was friendly were planning to go to South Africa during the summer break, and I naively assumed I would join these friends for this trip. The fact that I planned to join them put them in a quandary so the group assigned a good friend of mine the onerous task of informing me that I could not join them because of South Africa's apartheid policy. If I had gone, I would have been segregated from my colleagues for practically the entire trip.

I could not understand why some of my Peace Corps colleagues still would actually want to visit South Africa when they knew other Americans could not.

Of all the incidences that happened to me while I was a Volunteer, this was the hardest to bear as it illustrated for me the most blatant form of racism. At first I simply could not believe this policy actually existed as it seemed so ridiculous, but later I began to better understand the historical basis for the politics of that era and the struggle for the maintenance of power. But I also could not understand why some of my Peace Corps colleagues still would actually want to visit South Africa when they knew other Americans could not.

Brown like us! (1963)

While my friends chose to go to South Africa I decided to travel to Egypt. After returning to Asmara from spending a month where the sun shines all day, I didn't realize my skin color had changed from light yellow to a dark copper-tone brown until I returned to the classroom. And when I did, my students beamed with amazement with the statement that even startled me: "You're brown like us!"

In Asmara, I taught high school English at Haile Sellassie Secondary School using the simplified English version of numerous Reader's Digest books borrowed from the U.S. Informational Agency, and organized a school choral group.

DOUBLE DATE (1963)

One weekend while I was living in Asmara a Peace Corps colleague arranged a double date for the two of us with two soldiers from Kagnew Station, the American army communications' center located on the outskirts of the city. Only after it was too late did she and I realized that the second man — who was to be my dinner- and dancing-partner for the evening — had a venomous hatred of Asians. To help mitigate the possibility of an impending disaster and the awkwardness among us all, during the evening my friend's date talked with me and even danced with me, but my own date said not a word and pretended I was not there. I felt so uneasy that I abruptly demanded to be taken home.

ALMOST MEETING PREMIER CHOI ENLAI (1964)

During my second year of teaching Premier Choi Enlai from the People's Republic of China came to Asmara. One day, he was walking almost alone down the street where I happen to be walking my bicycle and I spotted him near the intersection where three streets converged. An American official nearby promptly told me not to wave at him, greet him, or acknowledge him in any other way. I surmised this was because of our

American policy towards China and our anti-communist stance. The situation was heightened even more because I was a Chinese American, and foreign journalists and other observers, including the Soviet Union, would have a field day taking photos and explaining U.S.-China relations if I actually did shake hands with the Premier.

CHUCK NORRIS AND BRUCE LEE IN ETHIOPIA (1992)

As an ethnomusicologist specializing in the music of Africa — Ethiopia and Eritrea in particular — I returned to Ethiopia a number of times. In 1992, I was invited to be a member of the official U.S. Election Observer Team to evaluate election procedures in 17 towns in Tigre, Ethiopia. A member of the observer team from Holland and I were paired up to travel together.

Because tight travel restrictions had been imposed from 1974 to 1991 throughout the country, Ethiopians had come to regard anyone from outside their own region as a foreigner. In the small towns where my fellow observer and I travelled, most Ethiopians only saw individuals from other countries via the media, and their perception of outsiders was shaped by movies, videos, and posters, as well as by hearsay, and as an Asian American woman traveling with a Dutch male colleague, we experienced some unusual reactions. At various times we were thought to be English, Italian, German, Russian, Japanese, and Chinese. We were even given the names of popular stars of martial arts films. This film genre was popular in Ethiopia because dialogue was secondary to the action and not critical to understanding the story line. Since these films were often the only exposure to Asians that rural Ethiopians experienced, they connected Asians with the martial arts that also reinforced racial stereotypes. My colleague was referred to as "Chuck Norris," and I was addressed as "Bruce Lee." Because I am female, Bruce Lee (pronounced "Bru-sah Lee" by Ethiopians) was sometimes altered to Rosa Lee (pronounced "Ro-sah Lee").

FINAL THOUGHTS

My Peace Corps experience has allowed me to view life from a broader perspective, and to have the belief that the impact of each Volunteer on his or her community may not always be apparent — even to the Volunteer.

Some experiences force Peace Corps Volunteers —
- to make independent decisions;
- to take a stand against injustices wherever and whenever they occur;
- to not be bitter about how one is treated because of ignorance and misconceptions;
- to realize that the way Americans conduct themselves abroad could have serious and unintended consequences.

We learn that —
- the policies of other countries advocating superiority of one group over another based on accident of birth and/or skin color should cause us to take stock of America's own civil rights history;
- the specter of prejudice can rear its ugly head at any time and anywhere, and it may not appear evident to others;
- the media is a powerful tool in exporting American culture influencing how others view us.

I was able —

- to observe the consequences of the United States involvement in foreign affairs even down to watching out of the corner of my eye the stereotypical Soviet-looking spies sitting in the local café bar we habituated — trench coats, sun glasses and all — listening to our conversations that must of driven them crazy;
- to learn about the United States from outsider perspectives;
- to reevaluate my own notions about African history, politics, religion, and the various art forms;
- to learn that successful students do not need all the physical trappings of education, but only excellent teachers who can speak about the topic at hand with passion, and who have an ability to improvise and teach without books, blackboards, desks and chairs; and that students who want to learn can learn even if they have to study under the street lights in the evening;
- to rediscover the joys of socializing in conversation and discussion while sipping bunna, chai, or tej;
- to enjoy a place where time unfolds at a slower pace that enables one to reflect, savor and replay in one's mind notable moments of the day.

Being passionate about what we did and compassionate toward the people with whom we worked were two factors that enabled us Peace Corps Volunteers to continue our work. It was under these circumstances that I began my lifelong interest in African music that prompted me to become an ethnomusicologist. Although music was not my official assignment as a Volunteer, on my own initiative, I learned the songs and dances of the

Although I have since studied other musics, none has had a greater impact on me than that first experience of hearing Ethiopian and Eritrean music in Africa.

Eritreans, and reciprocated by performing American music I knew including folk songs, popular songs, and square dances. In Asmara, I started and directed the high school choir. Although I have since studied other musics, none has had a greater impact on me than that first experience of hearing Ethiopian and Eritrean music in Africa.

One of the most common questions that I am asked about my Peace Corps service is what did I do and how did it help the Eritreans. In 1962 and 1963 I recorded Tigrinyan songs, and then transcribed twenty-three of them in written notation so I could study them. On a visit to Ethiopia in 2000, I played these songs to some of the young people I met in Addis Ababa and discovered they did not know these songs but some of their parents and grand parents did. A major reason the songs were not familiar to them was due, in part, to various political conflicts, most notably the 1974–91 revolution after Haile Selassie was overthrown by the Derg. During that time love songs, songs of a religious nature, and musical instruments associated with religion were banned in public and on the media, giving priority to songs of propaganda extolling the virtues of the regime.

The ban prompted me to have published some field recordings of pre-revolutionary music that I had made in 1972. This endeavor resulted in the UNESCO recording "Three Chordophone Traditions" being published in Germany in 1986 by Musicaphon, and being reissued by Auvidis in France in 1996. I wanted people — including Ethiopians and Eritreans living abroad — to be aware of this music.

> **I am returning these songs to the people who first gave them to me, and whom I was privileged to know in hopes that the next generation will learn and enjoy them, and pass them on.**

After the overthrow of the Derg in 1991, the ban was lifted. These Tirginyan songs with commentary and musical analysis, will be published as an historical document of an oral tradition of a certain place and time. One could say I am returning these songs[2] to the people who first gave them to me, and whom I was privileged to know in hopes that the next generation will learn and enjoy them, and pass them on.

Cynthia authored a longer version of this piece in part II of her essay titled: "Chance, Choice, and Opportunity: Effective Tools for Management," in /Management/ / Dynamic/s, Jaipuria Institute of Management. Lucknow, India. part II_ 2010, 10:1.

1　The Twentieth Century television series, "Ethiopia: The Lion and the Cross", Part 1, March 31, 1963 CBS (Season 6, Episode 20). Director/Script Harry Rasky. Host: Walter Cronkite, Reporter: Blaine Littell, Camera crew: British, Canadian, and French.

2　"Who Dared?": Twenty-two Təgərññya Songs from Mändäfära, Eritrea, /Papers of the 15th International Conference of Ethiopian Studies,/ Hamburg July 20-25, 2003. Siegbert Uhlig (ed.); Maria Bulakh, Denis Nosnitsin, and Thomas Rave (Assistant eds.). Harrassowitz Verlag, Wiesbaden, Germany. 2006: 446-458.

Another Real Adventure

BY MARY GRATIOT SCHULTZ (MENDEFERA 1965–1967)

SUNDAY, NOV 21, 1965

Dear Mom and Dad,

I went on another real adventure this weekend, to get a good picture of village life. Beanie, another Volunteer in my town, and I had planned to go to Adwa by horse and spend the night, but she got some infections all over her body. The doctor insisted that she come into Asmara. I decided that I still wanted to go someplace — and could use both of the horses.

Kesete

One of my students, Kesete Gebrekristos, had said that he lived in Kanafana. He had told me that he could not go home for a weekend because the buses didn't run frequently enough, or else he would have to walk 32 kilometers one way. So I asked him if he would like to ride to Kanafana with me, and I would stay with teachers there whom I had met on a previous visit.

We planned to leave at 6:30 AM on Saturday morning, but of course the students don't have clocks, and he was late. It was

7:45 by the time we left. Another student, Abraha, came with him to my house, but then Kesete left to go someplace, and said he would meet us on the road out of town. So Abraha got on one of the horses and started running him in the street. The horses have shoes that slide on the pavement. I called to him to stop running, but he didn't hear, and the horse fell all the way down on the pavement. Luckily, he didn't get hurt.

We finally got going and the horses really ran to the first village, Kude Felassie. Then I think they remembered how miserable they were crossing the desert area the last time we went to Kanafana, and we had a terrible time making them run. We wanted to get across the desert before it got too hot, but we didn't make it.

On the way we passed some nomads, a really strange sight — one family with all their belongings on one camel. Resting on the camel's hump was a six-foot square bed-like structure, made of a wood frame, with animal skins in the center. On this were the mother and grown daughter, and hanging from it, pots and many other unfamiliar objects. The father was leading the camel, and two sons were walking.

Also sighted along the way — a classic blue bus

Another strange sight were the ant hills. Some were as high as six feet.

About halfway to Kanafana, Kesete told me he didn't really live in Kanafana, but in another village that turned out to be about

5 kilometers away. He asked if I wanted to go to Kanafana or to his village first. The name of his village is Adi something which I can't attempt to spell or pronounce. Adi means village, by the way. I said we would go to his village since I thought he was probably anxious to get home to see his family. We turned off the road and had to walk the horses over terrible rocks (we were on the horses, but the horses were walking). The horses were very tired and hungry by this time.

We got to the village about 1 PM. We took the long path around the hill, instead of going over, because Kesete thought it would be easier for the horses. There were so many rocks that they still couldn't go very fast. All the houses in the village are exactly alike. They are made of rocks which are cut but not cemented together, and have a thatched roofs. They are rectangular, and actually pretty well built, with a wooden frame. In front of each house is a sort of fence to keep the hyenas away from the animals at night. The first room is for the larger animals — goats, mules and donkeys. The second and third rooms are much larger. There are no windows, so it seems quite dark inside even in the daytime.

The second room is the main living-sleeping-eating room. The beds are cement structures which come out of the wall, and look like tombs in the English cathedrals. Kesete slept on one of these beds, with a skin underneath (cowhide), but his parents slept on the floor.

When we got there, only Kesete's mother was home. He had written them a letter telling them that we were coming, and they certainly made preparations to receive me. I sat in the only chair, which was made from skins with a wooden frame, and they covered it with a cloth for me. First we had suwa, which I was afraid to drink, since I got sick from it the last time. Sometimes it tastes better than others, and this time it was not so good, so I didn't drink much. It is alcoholic, but if it is three or four days old, the effects are much less. Then we had zigini, which his mother made with not too much berbere for me. I am really getting to like zigini a lot now — after a week without it I get hungry for it. Then we had three hard-boiled eggs. The eggs are very cheap there, 2 for 5 cents (1 cent American per egg) but in Mendefera they are 5 cents each. His mother wanted me to take some to Mendefera, but I really couldn't carry them on the horse.

Then we had tea. By this time, Kesete's father, brother, brother's wife, and several other people had come to see me, all making speeches to me in Tigrinya, which Kesete translated. They welcomed me profusely, and said they liked America, and thanked me for coming to their village. The only other Americans to come to the village before this were two men on a mapping mission who landed their helicopter there for 15 minutes last year.

After we ate, we walked around the village for a while, and then took the horses to Kanafana, which is about 5 kilometers away. The path is just rocks, and we had to walk the horses all the way, so it took us 45 minutes.

We went to one of the teachers' houses. His name is Yemane. He lives alone, in an old school room. The only furniture was an American-type bed and two folding chairs. He has a sterno stove, and made scrambled eggs for us. You eat the eggs with a roll instead of a fork or spoon, and since the bread is hard, it's quite a trick to get the food in your mouth without spilling it. We also had beer and tea. The teacher insisted on feeding us although we were full from the zigini.

One of the other teachers came over also. The headmaster wasn't there, but I left a tape I had made for him with Yemane. Last time I was there he said he wanted some western music, so I recorded some for him using another Volunteer's tape recorder.

In Kanafana there are some shops — there are none in Kesete's village — so Kesete bought four rolls for our breakfast, and a bar of soap "so we can wash our hands and face in the morning."

We got back to Kesete's village just before dark, and it started to rain on the way back. People said that it has been raining every day, but this is very unusual for this time of year. When we got back, we went to visit his uncle and his brother's family. His brother's wife made tea for us. She has 6 or 7 children; the oldest is a boy of 15 who is in the first grade in Kanafana.

By this time it was completely dark. There was no moon, and I never knew it could be so dark! The oldest son carried a lantern for us back to Kesete's house, and spent the night there — he wanted to because I was there.

About 8 we had supper. Just Kesete and I ate together; the parents ate out of a separate dish. We had zigini with chicken, which is a real feast, and the chicken was killed in my honor.

We also had something like cottage cheese made from goat's milk — quite good, but I could get TB from it, so I didn't eat much. After eating, they bring a pan of water for washing your hands — the zigini always gets under your finger nails. I forgot to say that when I first arrived, the mother brought me a pan of water to wash my feet. Then many of the children from the village came to see me. Three were in sixth grade, and know some English, but were too shy to speak it.

We went to bed about 10, everyone in the same room. They said they were sorry they didn't have a separate room for me. I had brought a sleeping bag with me, but they got a bed for me — probably the only one in the village — made of a wooden frame with strips of hides woven across. About 20 chickens of all sizes were also sleeping in the room, and two cats were running around. After everyone was in bed, they talked for a while. The father is a priest, and since it was Sunday morning, he got up about 4 AM.

Mary at left with Kesete's family and neighbors

I really didn't sleep well — everyone was snoring and talking in their sleep. There were also bugs from someplace in my sleeping bag, and I'm covered with bites now. They were probably from the horse, because I had used the sleeping bag as a blanket, although I thought it was zipped and folded enough to keep them out. Next time I'll take my PC flea powder and insect repellent.

In the morning, we had tea, bread and eggs. I took pictures of Kesete with his mother and father, and several children and neighbors who appeared and wanted to be in the pictures; then Kesete took one of me with all these people. His mother put on her shama (stole), and his father is holding his fly swish and Coptic cross.

We left about 8, and, since the horses were going home, got back to Mendefera about noon.

Love, Mary

Saganeiti

The Saga of Saganeiti

BY PAUL E. HUNTSBERGER (SAGANEITI 1965–1967)

ON SEPTEMBER 11, 2001, I finally finished emailing students studying abroad with New Mexico State University to make sure they were safe, and to offer them help in responding to that day's national tragedy. Then I turned to my mail in-box and I saw a letter that I had been waiting for from the U.S.-OSEAS Partnership and Alumni Program cosponsored by the Educational Information and Resources Branch of the U.S. Department of State and Educational Testing Service. Nervously, I opened the letter and to my delight it was a notification that I had been selected to be an East Africa higher education short-term consultant to help the U.S. overseas educational advising centers in Malawi, Ethiopia, and Eritrea. At last, thirty-five years after departing Eritrea, where I had served as a Peace Corps Volunteer teacher from September 1965 to July 1967, I was returning to where my long international education career began.

I FIRST ARRIVED in Saganeiti on September 27, 1965. I had taken a bus from Asmara on a winding road that passed through Decamere — a medium-sized city that had a secondary school, and several small villages. The landscape consisted of rocky outcrops, scrubby bushes, and cactus. Upon entering Saganeiti, the other tired travelers and I saw a grove of tall, green eucalyptus trees. This impressive wood, maintained by the Forestry

Department for research, stood out because trees were not plentiful in northern Ethiopia.

At that time Saganeiti was said to have about 2,000 residents who dwelled at 7,500 feet above sea level in a valley nestled among the many rugged mountains that surrounded it. It was 40 miles south of Asmara, the provincial capital, on the south-easterly road that continued on to Addis Ababa via Adi Caieh, Senafe and Mekele.

The bus stopped in the village square that had a post office (with the only telephone in the community), a gas station, an Italian restaurant and hotel, and two houses. One was home to Virginia — Ginger — Vieser, a second-year Peace Corps Volunteer who was the other Peace Corps teacher assigned to the middle school where I would teach. Her house had electricity at night from 6 to 11 if the town generator functioned properly, two bedrooms, a big kitchen with a kerosene stove, and a small bathroom with a squat-type toilet and a cold-water shower. It also had a kerosene-operated refrigerator, a luxury that I came to cherish over the two years I stayed in Saganeiti. The two of us arranged that I would take my meals at her house.

My three-room house had a cold-water shower and erratic electricity at night — as was the case in the entire village. The house was located on the other side of the village from the base of the hill that led up to our school. Over time I lost a lot of weight walking up that hill twice daily, and across town three times daily for my meals at Ginger's. (When she returned to the U.S. in 1966, I took over her house and her replacement, Bob Brown, shared the house with me.)

Following my arrival, a Peace Corps driver came to Saganeiti to deliver my personal belongings, and he drove me up to the school, and to the hilltop above that commanded a panoramic view of the village.

The Peace Corps driver and Paul in the rear with the welcoming committee

Word spread rapidly that I had arrived. I was enthusiastically surrounded by the children of the town who were eager to see the new teacher who had come to replace Ken Hatcher, the highly respected PCV who had completed his two-year term as a teacher several months earlier. Ken and I had met during my group's training at UCLA, but we did not know at the time that I would be his replacement. The children shouted out "salam" and shook my hand. Salam was the only word I understood, because Volunteers assigned to serve in Eritrea had been taught Amharic in training (in 1965 Eritrea was a province of Ethiopia and Amharic was the country's official language). I hoped the enthusiasm of the students would continue when I began teaching.

Ginger introduced me to our maid, Berekti Andu, who was tasked with preparing our meals, doing our laundry by hand, cleaning the house, and shopping for vegetables and a goat at the weekly outdoor market. She would have the goat butchered, and it became our main source of meat as the key ingredient in the spicy stew called zigini. I came to rely on Berekti to teach me Tigrinya, and to advise me on the mores and customs of the people of Saganeiti. About age 50, she was an amazing women

Berekti became a special person in my life and I thought of her not as a maid, but as my Eritrean mother who counseled me as I learned to adjust to life in Saganeiti.

who had never attended school yet spoke Tigrinya, Amharic, English, Italian, and Arabic — all because she had worked for families who spoke these languages. Berekti became a special person in my life and I thought of her not as a maid, but as my Eritrean mother who counseled me as I learned to adjust to life in Saganeiti.

Ginger took me to the school on the second day I was in Saganeiti to meet the headmaster and teachers, and we found out that it would be 10 days before classes started.

That afternoon a student named Iyub took me on a guided tour of the town, and the old Italian fort built on an escarpment overlooking it. The long walk up the mountain road was arduous but the sight was breathtaking. I later came to this secluded spot many times to read, rest, and think. As we walked, Iyub quickly loosened up and talked freely with me in excellent English. He said that Eritrea did not want to be a colony of Ethiopia. I heard this revolutionary sentiment pronounced daily by many of the students, and I had to be diplomatic in my reactions to protect my neutral status as a PCV.

Soon after arriving I noticed that students and teachers found it difficult to pronounce my Germanic-origin name, and finally I decided to make it easier for everyone. I took on the name Ato Paulos, or Mr. Paul (Paulos being a Biblical name familiar to many Eritreans).

I started to learn basic Tigrinya and I quickly mastered the characters (as I had done with Amharic in training), so I could write it. But I had no access to books or tapes for learning to speak the language, so I relied on Berekti, the children of the town, and the students to teach me. Village children loved to come to my house to play games (I taught them to throw a frisbee and they taught me traditional Eritrean games), to eat roasted chick peas, and to gossip in elementary Tigrinya about various town folks. The students made sure I knew all the insults and other useful words and phrases. I also picked up some basic Italian.

The Italian influence on Eritrea and Saganeiti was evident everywhere. As mentioned, the Italians had built the fort up on the escarpment as it was strategic high ground for military purposes during World War II. I was told that the middle school had been an Italian military hospital during the Italian occupation. A local Catholic mission was operated by priests from Italy, and the restaurant/hotel located in the center of town across from Ginger's house was owned by an Italian. Some Italians and Eritreans intermarried, and a number of villagers, especially the merchants, spoke Italian.

FINALLY THE SCHOOL YEAR BEGAN on October 6, and Ginger came to me and said she had a very special 8th grade student whom she thought had tremendous innate ability, and could make something of himself if he would develop discipline and work harder. She wanted him to do extra study to prepare to apply for a scholarship to General Wingate Secondary School in Addis Ababa. This would be a full scholarship that covered all expenses for four years, and no student from Saganeiti had ever received this scholarship.

I agreed to help her motivate this student, Simon Gebredingil. I met with him and told him that if he would agree to be tutored

Simon's first airplane ride

to prepare for the scholarship competition, and then earned the scholarship, I would pay for an all-expenses trip by airplane for him to travel to Addis Ababa and Jimma. Simon accepted the challenge, diligently applied himself, and won the scholarship. And in the summer of 1966 Simon took his first airplane ride — this started him on the road to success. He wrote to me regularly after he arrived at General Wingate, and later when he had to leave Addis because of riots and animosity toward Eritreans. We kept in touch by letter through 1970, even though I lived in Ohio, Pennsylvania, Alabama, India, Iowa, California, New York, Connecticut and back to Ohio after leaving Eritrea in 1967. I never forgot about Simon, and always wished to find out what had happened to him. I knew he had become active in the independence movement, and hoped that he was still alive.

THE SAGANEITI MIDDLE SCHOOL was constructed of rocks that were covered with plaster on the inside, and stucco on the outside. The classrooms were spacious and each had three open windows for light. Fortunately the sun shone brightly most days as the school had no electricity in the classrooms. The roof was made of corrugated metal which, I learned soon enough, rattled so loudly during a rainstorm that all teaching had to cease until the rain stopped. Each room had one 6 by 6 foot blackboard that was well-worn and difficult to write on with chalk. The common practice for teachers was to write a lesson on the board, have the students copy the material, and then memorize it. And the students were experts at memorizing. Give them a test asking for one word from their notes, and they would write three sentences preceding and three following that one word.

I was assigned to teach 6th grade English, world history, geography, and Ethiopian history. I had taught English and social studies in a rural high school in Ohio, so I was prepared for world history and geography. But I knew little about teaching English as a second language. I knew less about Ethiopian history. Fortunately I had a book on Ethiopian history that I read to keep a day ahead of the students who, frankly, didn't care to learn too much Ethiopian history, but were always eager in class to have the opportunity to denounce Ethiopian imperialism. We had no book for world history and geography. "Too expensive," the headmaster told me.

My second year I insisted that I teach only all 7th and 8th grade English classes because Bob Brown, who came that year, was a science teacher, and I felt I could teach English better than any of the other teachers, none of whom were native English speakers.

I had anticipated that I would have few, if any, teaching aids or materials in Eritrea. When I taught high school in rural Ohio, I had learned to develop my own teaching materials — which I felt were better than the outdated books the Ohio school still used. Peace Corps provided us with a Gestetner alcohol-spirit copy machine, and I had a typewriter, so I created and printed my own teaching materials. These I handed out to the students to keep, so they wouldn't waste so much class time copying from the blackboard, and this gave more time for discussion and for practice in speaking English.

Posters on the classroom wall

Using lots of photographs I had cut out from old history books I had obtained, I made posters. Then, when I talked about social, economic, or political conditions elsewhere in the world about which the students had no frame of reference, they could look at the pictures depicting life in other countries. I hung the posters on the classroom walls, and students from other classes had the opportunity to look at and read them each day as well.

For teaching English, I came across a publication from the UK on Teaching English as a Second Language that stressed teaching language patterns without emphasizing memorization of grammar rules. The point was for the students to learn English as a child would before being required to learn grammar during formal schooling. Daily I presented a pattern, such as the past tense, and showed the pattern and how the students could plug in words to fill in the pattern. Then I made sure that every day every student spoke in class. I taught them to communicate in English, not to memorize rules.

I also tried to instill in the students the perspective that, yes their school may have limited facilities and materials, but they could achieve with personal effort in spite of this. I came from a poor family and attended a small middle school and high school in rural Ohio. Yet I had earned a bachelor's degree from the private College of Wooster, and had completed all but the thesis for a master's degree at Vanderbilt University. So I tried to inspire them to look inside themselves to develop pride in learning all they could, and to work hard in and out of class. In addition, I encouraged them to ask questions and to enter into discussions from different viewpoints. Most local teachers lectured or wrote information on the blackboards for students to copy, but they did not encourage the students to talk and express their viewpoints. A method I used while teaching high school in Ohio was to have students ask questions and express opinions (but they had to know what had influenced the development of their opinions). My Ohio students told me that I was the only teacher during their four years of high school who valued and respected what they had to say. The Eritrean students appreciated this method too.

EARLY IN THE FIRST SEMESTER, I learned that the school had a small library with only a limited number of books, and it was never opened to the students. The headmaster felt that the students would take the books or deface them.

I also noticed that the two and one-half hour lunch break was way too long — the students didn't do anything constructive with the free time. I started talking to the students who said this long break was a waste of time. I suggested to them that I was willing to come back to school early after lunch and help them with their assignments and tutor them in English.

Finally, I also learned that the students had compulsory physical education, but all they did was do marching drills, and never were taught to play any games — although all of them could play football.

I began to think about the Peace Corps requirement that during summer break all Volunteers had to participate in some type of community service activity. Peace Corps had organized many projects such as immunizing against polio and smallpox, mostly in southern Ethiopia, but I wanted to stay in Saganeiti. I contacted our local Peace Corps administrator for Eritrea and asked if I could organize and implement my own project in Saganeiti. The answer was yes — as long as the project was submitted for approval.

What I proposed was a project that would address three needs of the student population of Saganeiti: 1) obtain more books for the library, and open it for student use, 2) conduct summer school classes, and 3) organize sports activities that made coming to school fun. My proposal was approved.

For my first objective I needed to obtain lots of books and other reading materials to supply the library so I decided to conduct a book drive in cooperation with a teacher in Ohio who had been my student-teaching supervisor. A... group of student volunteers, who would be overseen by one of the teachers, could organize the library, and open it every day at lunchtime so students could practice their English, and have a quiet place to study.

Second, since the students did not attend school in the summer, and many of them did not work or have any other obligations, many wanted to continue learning during the long break between academic sessions. I proposed the development of a summer school staffed by other Peace Corps Volunteer friends who could come to Saganeiti to complete their summer service obligation. I was able to recruit three Volunteers who agreed to conduct tutoring in English two to three hours per day, and to teach students how to play basketball and volleyball once we built the facilities.

For the third objective — because the school had no athletic facilities, I proposed that the students and I, along with other community volunteers, build and erect basketball backboards, install posts for a volleyball net, and convert the area where students marched into a basketball court and a volleyball court.

MY FIRST TWO OBJECTIVES were attained with great success. My teacher friend in Ohio organized a Books for Africa drive that resulted in many cartons of books and magazines being donated by school children in Ohio and that were sent to the students of Saganeiti. The library was stocked, and student volunteers opened it on a daily basis —and all books and magazines were treated with respect by the students so that others could use them.

Studying in the revitalized library

Summer school was conducted with many students coming every day to be tutored in English, and any other subjects they wanted to study. These students were also allowed to use the library.

MY THIRD OBJECTIVE REQUIRED some special effort to attain. Since we needed some money to buy lumber, hardware, paint, nets, balls, etc., the students suggested that they perform a drama for the town and charge a modest entrance fee. At about the same time the Provincial Educational Director had come to visit the school, and I told him about this project and the enthusiasm of the students. He agreed to provide any money we still might need after the fund raising event.

The students put on a great drama and dance show in the spring of 1966 for the community, and the effort generated a nice sum of money for the sports project. The Ministry came through with the balance that was needed.

The basketball and volleyball courts were built during the summer with the help of the visiting Volunteers. The students were amazed that Peace Corps teachers could work with their hands and didn't mind getting dirty.

On the new basketball court

Starting in the summer and continuing into fall of 1966, games were played every day. In fact, some students came early to school to shoot baskets, and stayed after school to play volleyball.

As part of this third project I had proposed that the school be divided into teams, and that everybody had to play — including the teachers, who would play against the students at various times throughout the year. The students were ecstatic with this arrangement.

THE SPORTS SEGMENT of the project was brought to the attention of people at Kagnew U.S. Military Base in Asmara, and staff at the base school for dependents of the military personnel asked if they could bring their students from the school down to Saganeiti to play basketball against our students as a way to help their children learn about the country in which their parents were serving and they were living.

The Saganeiti Basketball Team, with Coach Bob Brown in front

Bob Brown, the Peace Corps Volunteer who had replaced Ginger in September of 1966, was a good athlete, and he agreed to build and coach a team of our best players.

The game was played in Saganeiti between our students and the Kagnew school students, and was witnessed by many in the village. Then the Kagnew folks, who had so much fun and learned a lot about Eritreans, invited our team to travel to the base to play their team in their modern gymnasium.

After that game, our students slept on cots in the gymnasium and went to the mess hall to eat breakfast with the Kagnew students and others. This trip was the talk of the town (even though we lost), and was a once-in-a-lifetime opportunity for the students. They showed that they wanted to improve their school and themselves, and to learn about a bigger world. I was teaching them that learning doesn't happen only in the classroom, and that a good idea backed by hard work pays off.

ANOTHER OBSERVATION I HAD MADE about the school was that many students attended school during the week and stayed in crammed sleeping rooms. Then they returned to their villages that were from three to ten miles away for the weekend. I liked to walk, and I felt that I should become more aware of the communities from which our students came, so I asked various students if they would take me to their villages on the weekends. They were delighted to do this and during the fall of 1965 and the spring of 1966 I walked to their villages, slept in their families' modest homes made of mud and tree branches and rocks, ate meals of shiro (a porridge with spices), raw honey, bread (taita), and what ever else they had to share. The parents I met were proud that their children's teacher had come to their homes, and they beamed when I gave them a gift of coffee beans and sugar (Berekti's suggestion) — commodities hard to obtain in the remote villages. I always took photos of each family and their village, and I had prints made to give them a copy as a thank you gift. For most families this was the first, and maybe only time, they had been photographed. What impressed me most when I made these visits was how these poor and humble people shared the best of what they had, tried to make me welcomed and comfortable under limited conditions, and wanted their

One of the families with whom Paul visited

sons to succeed in their studies so they could have a better life. The students told me that no teacher, Eritrean or PCV, had ever taken the time to walk to their villages to meet with their families.

Several times when I visited a student's home in a remote village I was impressed that I saw hanging on the wall of a modest home a picture of President John F. Kennedy provided by the U.S. Information Service. The people were deeply grateful to President Kennedy for establishing the Peace Corps and providing hundreds of teachers to their country. They felt that they had lost a brother when he was assassinated. One of my Eritrean students, who saw a Life magazine I had brought to my house that showed Kennedy's funeral at Arlington, said to me in Tigrinya: "Why is it other Kings die, and so young, but our father (Emperor Haile Selassie) still lives." Yet again, the depth of Eritrean despair over Ethiopian rule came out into the open in front of me. Clearly, as I wrote in my diary, something was brewing and would soon openly manifest itself.

IN SEPTEMBER 1966 the campaign for independence intensified. On the first night after I returned from summer vacation, the police station in Saganeiti was attacked by rebels who ran between the Post Office and my house as they fled from the village. Soon a curfew was enforced from dusk to dawn. Then the busses going to and from Asmara had armed escorts of army trucks mounted with machine guns. Finally the Ethiopian army encamped at the old Italian fort on the hill above Saganeiti. They made regular sorties by helicopters to search for the rebels, a sight that became common in the sky above the village. My idyllic days of walking up to the fort for rest and relaxation came to an abrupt end, as did the treks I took with students to Digsa, Ewanet, Adengeform, and Acrur. One September day the Ethiopian army stopped me and some students while we walked outside Saganeiti, and I was told that I could not walk to the students' villages for security reasons. The students told me that the soldiers thought I might be a spy.

Volleyball after school

DURING THE ACADEMIC year of 1966–1967, I had to content myself with just staying engaged in Saganeiti and enjoying the rhythm of life that I had come to revere: teaching and playing volleyball with students after school; entertaining the village children with games and snacks; participating in festivals such as the Feast of Saint Michael; attending weddings and even a funeral of the new headmaster who died suddenly of hepatitis in the fall 1966 (I had sent him to Decamere to seek medical treatment as I recognized he was jaundiced and ill); sharing zigini and tej (honey wine) and playing cards with teacher friends who risked a beating by soldiers when they left after the start of curfew to go home (sometimes I made them stay the night at my house); and visiting Berekti's brother and sister to enjoy coffee prepared traditionally.

Berekti and Paul

BEFORE I KNEW IT, year two came to an end. I said my good-byes to Berekti, who gave me a gift of a jabena, a traditional coffee pot, she had a potter make specially for me; to the teachers, I gave them books from the Booklocker, the footlocker of books that Peace Corps had provided for the Volunteers; to the new headmaster, a Moslem named Mohammed who gave me his personal prayer mat as a gift; and to many students, some of whom came to the airport in Asmara to wish me farewell. I told them all I would try to return, but never thought so many years would pass before the Saganeiti saga continued.

Now FOR THE REST OF THE STORY.

In the spring of 1999, I received a call from the Health Science Department at New Mexico State University where I have worked as Assistant Director of International Programs since 1981. I was asked to review two applications for undergraduate admission from two older students from Eritrea. I reviewed their documents, and verified that some papers were missing because the country had been at war and they could have been destroyed or lost. And I added that I had taught Eritrean students whom I found to be intelligent, diligent in their studies, and spoke good English. I recommended that these two older students be given a chance to attend New Mexico State University based on their professional experiences, and their selection by the U.S. Agency for International Development for scholarships. The department accepted my recommendation to admit these two students.

I thought no more about this until one day in September when I saw two students coming into the building where I worked, and I knew they hailed from Eritrea. I always made a point of greeting students from Africa, and I walked up to them and asked if they were from Eritrea. They smiled and said "Yes, how did you know this?" I said that I had been expecting two new students from Eritrea and thought they might be those students — which they were. I asked them what city they came from, and the first, Tareke, said "Adi Caieh." I told him that I had visited Adi Caieh, but I didn't know anyone from there. The second student, Tecle, said he came from Saganeiti! I said that I knew Saganeiti very well and that I had taught there. He asked me my name, and I started to say Dr. Huntsberger, but I paused and then said, "My name is Ato Paulos." He looked at me intently and then said that he knew me. He was in the eighth grade during the 1965–66 school year, and his English teacher had been Ginger Vieser. He remembered that I had taught there too, and that I had organized the sports programs for students. Now I was excited, and I asked for his apartment address and email address. I said that I would be inviting them to come to my house for dinner.

It wasn't until Thanksgiving that I was able to offer the invitation. Tecle and Tareke met my family, and after dinner I asked them if they would like to look at some slides I had taken while I lived in Saganeiti. I showed them pictures of the school and students, and they recognized many of them. I asked if they knew a student named Zerzghi Sbhatu, whom I had mentored during my second year of Peace Corps service, and who had won the General Wingate Secondary School scholarship that year. They said that he had been killed during the war.

Then I said I had one special slide I wanted to show them, and it was the picture of Simon Gebredingil boarding the Ethiopian Airlines plane in Jimma, the last stop on the trip I had promised him when he won his scholarship to Wingate School. I asked: "Do you know him?" "Yes," Tecle said, "he is a good friend." "Is he alive?" I asked. "Yes, and he works for the Government of Eritrea in the Ministry of Security." Tecle promised to find his address so I could contact him.

I wrote to Simon, and in December 1999 I received a letter from him, the first one since 1970. He said: "When I came back after the war, among the few personal belongings that I found with my parents was a 29-year-old letter from Ato Paulos. And when I heard from you again this week, I was deeply moved." Now part of the circle had been closed, but I still needed to find a way to travel to Eritrea to see Simon and other students, and to connect with Berekti, if she were still alive.

I HAD LEARNED ABOUT THE OSEAS Partnership Program when I hosted some educational advisors from Mexico, Malawi, Thailand and the Philippines who were visiting NMSU to learn about the U.S. educational system. During the that visit, they told me that OSEAS also had a reciprocal program for U.S. educators that allowed them to travel to consult at various advising centers around the world.

In the spring of 2001 I heard that the program wanted to invite a university administrator with a Ph. D. who could consult at overseas advising centers in Ethiopia, Malawi and Eritrea, and I jumped at the chance to apply. As soon as I was confirmed and knew my itinerary, I contacted Simon and told him I would be going to Eritrea in February 2002. That January I received a fax from him that said: "Ato Paulos travel to Eritrea after about 35 years! I can feel the excitement to find so many things: people and places, very different due to the enormous change . . . ." He invited me to visit him and his family. Previously I had asked him if he knew the whereabouts of Berekti Andu, but he said that he had no idea if she were still alive.

ON FEBRUARY 5, 2002, I DEPARTED from Las Cruces, New Mexico, to begin my return journey to Eritrea — the first leg of my six-week trip to three African countries. While preparing to leave my house for the airport, I told my wife that I had a premonition that Berekti was alive and that somehow I would find her. How, I didn't know, but I planned to use my Rotarian connections to assist in the effort. I was President of my Rotary Club from 2001 to 2002, so I arranged with Eden Zerastion, the advisor at the Overseas Advising Center in the U. S. Embassy in Asmara, who was to be my host, to arrange for me to attend a Rotary meeting in Asmara on February 7. Maybe by a remote chance a Rotarian would have information about Berekti.

I arrived in Asmara on February 6. The next day I attended several meetings, and then was driven to the hotel where the Asmara Rotary Club was having its weekly meeting. I signed in as a visiting Rotarian and told the club I was the President of a club in New Mexico. They asked me to say a few words to their club about my club, which I did. Then I added that I had a question for the audience: "Was anybody born and raised in Saganeiti?" I said that I had been a Peace Corps teacher there, and I was know as Ato Paulos. No one raised a hand or said anything. I felt that I may have failed in my attempt to find information about people who lived in Saganeiti, including Berekti Andu.

As I was paying for the meal after the meeting ended, a businessman named Keflemariam approached me and said: "I didn't put up my hand when you asked the question since I was not born or raised in Saganeiti, but I know it well. In fact, didn't you hire a woman named Berekti?" My knees went weak and I said: "Do you mean Berekti Andu?" He said "Yes." I eagerly asked him if she was still alive. If so, she would have to be in her mid-80s — quite old for those living in Africa, and I had heard during my earlier meetings that Saganeiti had been at the center of fighting during the war, and feared that she might have been killed. Keflemariam said that she was alive, but frail, and living in Asmara. He asked when I could see her, and we agreed to meet on Sunday morning.

When I returned to the hotel there was a message that Simon had been trying to contact me. I called his home and he said that he would be right over to see me. As soon as I saw him I recognized him even though he had been a teenager when I saw him last. As we talked he told me that his Peace Corps teachers had a profound influence on him, and that the English he learned from me and the other teachers convinced him to become serious about education so that he could improve his lot in life.

Berekti and Paul, 2002

ON SUNDAY, I MET BEREKTI ANDU, the 86-year-old maid and Eritrean mother whom I had know for two years. She had lost most of her English, but she said in Tigrinya "You sure have gotten old." "So have you," I laughed remembering how we used to speak so directly and honestly to each other. We talked for about an hour before she had to leave, and I was on cloud nine to know Berekti was alive and well. Berekti never thought she would see any of the Peace Corps Volunteers she worked for, and she was thrilled to see me again. Eden Zerastion, who had asked to come to the reunion with Berekti, said that she was amazed that I had such real feelings for a maid, which was not common in Eritrean society. I said she was more than a maid to me — she was family.

With Simon and his family

ON MONDAY AND TUESDAY I had the opportunity to visit Simon at his home and meet his family and to meet other students who had learned I was in Asmara. Two of them were Afewerki and Hailemariam.

Afewerki had fought in the war. Haile-mariam had polio as a child and he was crippled when I first knew him. I was impressed with his tenacity. He reminded me that I had given him a women's bike so that he could get around Saganeiti more easily since walking was difficult for him. He became a dermatologist and ran a clinic in Addis Ababa, but when the war began, he lost it and was required to return to Eritrea. They also told me that Gebrehewit, whom I had hired to be a house boy to help with errands to help him pay his school and living expenses, had an advanced degree and was working either for the UN or some other development organization.

What these students remembered most about Peace Corps was how the teachers helped them to learn English, and how they inspired them to improve by getting their education.

What these students remembered most about Peace Corps was how the teachers helped them to learn English, and how they inspired them to improve by getting their education. They remembered me as a very friendly person, but one who was very serious as a teacher and who was well organized and able to teach subjects clearly and thoroughly. I felt great that we Volunteers who taught in Saganeiti — Ken, Ginger, Bob, I and others — had a significant influence on these Eritrean leaders and professionals.

BEFORE I LEFT ERITREA for Malawi, I traveled to Saganeiti. Coming into Saganeiti I saw two burned out tanks that were left in place to be reminders of the war. The area, because of its strategic location, had been at the heart of the fighting. Many of the eucalyptus trees had been cut down during the war, but new trees — "martyr trees" — had been planted by national service workers. Saganeiti had grown. The house in the center had been destroyed and now was rebuilt as a hotel. My first house near the school had been damaged, but the new owner was remodeling it for his family. What we had built at the school was now gone.

I WAS SCHEDULED TO LEAVE Eritrea on February the 14th and the night of February 13th, after returning late from meetings and visits to schools and ministry offices, I arrived at my hotel. Waiting for me was Tecle, one of the students from NMSU, who had graduated in 2001, and had been recognized as the Outstanding International Graduate at graduation ceremonies that I had attended. He had returned to Eritrea to work in educating communities about AIDS. He wanted to take me out to dinner, but I asked that we have dinner in the hotel since I was tired and needed to pack as I was leaving for Malawi the next day. He agreed, and after washing up, I sat down with him. Then Simon arrived to join us and continue the reunion.

A couple minutes after sitting down, a waiter came over to me and said a lady wanted to see me. I asked him to point her out, and it was Berekti. She had walked from her home to the hotel in the dark so that she could see me one more time, and give me a gift of a colorful basket. I walked over to greet her and insisted that she join us for dinner. I was proud to have dinner with my former students and my Eritrean mother as my last remembrance of Eritrea.

While I doubt that I will return again to Eritrea, I still try to keep in touch with Simon. For a while Eden kept in touch with Berekti for me, and she has become my Eritrean sister. Just two months after I returned from Africa, she visited me in New Mexico. She was in Santa Fe for a conference, and I drove 600 miles round trip to pick her up and take her to my home for the weekend, and then returned her to Santa Fe. Eden is now living in the U.S. where her husband is a student. Recently I saw her in Seattle at a conference.

I will never forget my debt to the people of Eritrea for changing my life, as I know I helped some of them to change their lives.

In the last year I have had two other former students contact me. One was a student to whom I had given some money so he could pay his rent and not drop out of school, and he went on to finish college and became a judge. The other is one of the students who took me to his village to meet his family. He lives in San Jose, California. I sent him photos I scanned from the hundreds of colored slides I have kept, and he was pleased to show his family pictures of his father and sister and scenes of his village that his children have never seen. We are committed to keeping in touch as I will never forget my debt to the people of Eritrea for changing my life, as I know I helped some of them to change their lives.

Made in the USA
Lexington, KY
25 August 2012